The Atlas of
LOST
CITIES

The Atlas of LOST CITIES

Legendary cities rediscovered

BRENDA ROSEN

 A GODSFIELD BOOK

An Hachette Livre UK Company

First published in Great Britain in 2007
by Godsfield Press
a division of Octopus Publishing Group Ltd
2–4 Heron Quays, London E14 4JP
www.octopusbooks.co.uk

Distributed in the United States and Canada by
Sterling Publishing Co., Inc.
387 Park Avenue South, New York, NY 10016-8810

ISBN: 978-1-84181-327-1

A CIP catalogue record for this book is available from the
British Library.

Printed and bound in China

10 9 8 7 6 5 4 3 2 1

CONTENTS

Introduction

The first civilizations of the world developed about 5,500 years ago on the floodplain between the Tigris and Euphrates Rivers in what is now Iraq. The development of cities is agreed by historians and archeologists to be an indication that a tribe, chiefdom or other early form of social organization has evolved into a civilization. The word 'civilization' itself comes from the Latin civitas, meaning 'city'.

Right Relief carvings on the Apadana (audience hall) at Persepolis, Iran, show a procession of representatives of the nations conquered by Cyrus the Great to create the Persian Empire, bearing gifts of tribute to the king.

Certain recognizable characteristics seem to have been shared by the ancient cities. Their society was organized into distinct classes based on occupation, such as agricultural workers, craftspeople and artisans, merchants, soldiers and rulers and their kin. These classes generally shared a set of political and religious beliefs and accepted collective civic norms and responsibilities, such as laws and taxes. Cities often expressed their beliefs through the construction of monumental public works, from water distribution and sewage systems to palaces, municipal buildings, temples and public artworks. Many early cities were unified by a standardized monetary system and by a system of commerce through which they could interact with other cities via trade. Finally, the elite inhabitants of many early cities held common cultural and intellectual knowledge, such as systems of writing, arithmetic, geometry and astronomy.

'The word "civilization" comes from the Latin civitas, meaning "city".'

A city's setting and natural environment also played a central role in its development over the years. One key factor was the availability of natural resources, such as water for agriculture or useful and precious minerals, such as copper, tin, flint, silver and gold, for industry and trade. Other important factors that influenced the growth of early cities were helpful weather patterns, such as favourable annual rainfall, irrigating floods and predictable trade winds, as well as access to harbours, rivers or overland trade routes and the geographic proximity of friendly trading partners. Ancient cities were also stimulated by population increases caused by rising birth rates, migration and the conquest and assimilation of populations through war. As you will discover, all these different circumstances played a part in the rise of the ancient cities discussed in this book.

WHY ANCIENT CITIES COLLAPSED

Like the factors that stimulated the growth of cities, the circumstances that contributed to their decline and fall also have common themes. Some ancient cities flourished for centuries, while others were lost to the sea, the desert or the jungle, or were destroyed by natural disasters or the depredations of war. Why did some cities thrive and others fail? And what can we learn from the collapse of ancient cities to help us keep our own cities flourishing into the future?

Social scientists have identified four sets of factors that have influenced the collapse of ancient cities. Let us look at some examples of each.

NATURAL CLIMATE CHANGES

The first set of factors involves a natural change in a city's weather or climate. The survival of an early city depended on its ability to provide the necessities of life for the people who inhabited it. Over a period of time, the climate of a city can become hotter or colder, wetter or drier, because of natural variations that have little to do with human behaviour. Changing rainfall and temperature patterns, volcanic eruptions that filled the atmosphere with dust and allowed less sunlight to reach Earth, and natural erosion that changed the course of rivers or altered the coastline have all contributed to the collapse of ancient cities.

Though early cities could do nothing to prevent such natural climatic fluctuations, human behaviour did affect whether climate change had devastating consequences. Short human lifespans and long cycles of climatic variations meant that, after several decades of favourable conditions, people tended to forget what could happen during less favourable periods. Population growth and increased agricultural production in good years meant more mouths to feed, and less virgin land to cultivate, when climatic conditions turned unfavourable.

Unfortunately, a similar amnesia affects some modern cities. When periods of ample rainfall fill reservoirs, city populations in warmer and drier regions explode. When rainfall decreases and water supplies start to

Above As the great Taklamakan Desert expanded, the oasis cities of the Silk Road, such as Loulan, were gradually swallowed by shifting sand dunes.

massive earthquake and tsunami. Stories like these were made even more relevant by the accounts broadcast around the world of the tsunami of 26 December 2004 that battered coastlines in India and South-East Asia, and of the devastation of New Orleans by Hurricane Katrina in 2005. Modern technology, it seems, can do little to minimize the destructive power of such natural catastrophes.

DAMAGE TO THE ENVIRONMENT

The people who lived in ancient cities were just as prone as we are today to causing inadvertent damage to their environment. Deforestation to clear land for agriculture or provide timber for construction, over-fishing and hunting, farming practices that depleted the soil and other types of environmental damage were not mistaken 'policies' carried out by societies that were indifferent to their environment. Rather, they were the unforeseen and, in some cases, tragic consequences of the unrestricted human use of natural resources.

Human-caused environmental damage was a contributory factor in the decline of many of the cities described in this book. For example, when the Mayan population of Copán began to build homes and grow crops on the steep hills surrounding the city, deforestation of the slopes led to unchecked erosion. Not only was the fragile soil of the hills depleted of nutrients, but rainwater run-off also carried depleted sediment down into the valley where it covered more fertile fields, reducing their yields. Similarly, cities whose agriculture depended on irrigation from nearby rivers were vulnerable to flooding, as happened in Mohenjo-Daro in Pakistan, or to a fall in crop yield in the case of prolonged drought, as happened in Ur in ancient Mesopotamia.

Today, many scientists say that the most potent environmental threat is global warming caused by the release of carbon dioxide and other gases into the atmosphere. The stories of ancient sea-coast cities lost to rising sea levels, such as Mahabalipuram in India and Herakleion in Egypt, provide an insight into the current

dwindle away, wildfires, municipal water shortages and agricultural catastrophes create headlines. When we read about how cities of the past thrived or died because of natural climate changes, it is worth asking ourselves how an unfavourable change in the climate would affect the cities of today.

Another cause of the collapse of cities, related to the natural fluctuations in the climate described above, is the devastation wreaked by natural disasters such as floods, storms, earthquakes, tsunamis and volcanic eruptions. There are harrowing accounts of many such disasters in this book: cities like Knossos, whose elegant palaces were shaken to the ground by earthquakes; Pompeii, buried under tons of pumice and ash by the eruption of Mount Vesuvius; and Port Royal in Jamaica, destroyed in a few hours by a

debate about this problem. Scientists have warned that the Arctic may be free of summer ice as soon as 2040. The dramatic rise in ocean levels that may result threatens sea-coast cities around the world. In Shanghai and the surrounding area, for instance, a rise of 5.5–6 metres (18–20 feet) in sea levels would force more than 40 million people to abandon their homes.

WAR

Many of the ancient cities in this book were lost as a result of attacks by hostile neighbours or invasions from distant civilizations. Wars were frequent occurrences for early civilizations, as is demonstrated by the walls, moats and other fortifications that encircled many cities of the time. Such defensive measures gave ancient people a sense of security and helped stronger cities to survive repeated attacks. When the Vandals captured Leptis Magna on the coast of North Africa, they destroyed the city's walls, leaving it vulnerable. Less than a

hundred years later the city was sacked by the Berbers. However, even a city with excellent fortifications could not hold out permanently against a determined enemy, as was demonstrated by the fall of Troy and of the Aztec capital, Tenochtitlan.

As historians have pointed out, cities that succumbed to external attack had often already been weakened by internal problems. Climate changes, environmental damage, religious and political disputes, epidemics and other internal difficulties made cities more susceptible to enemy conquest. For instance, the shift that was made from Hinduism to Theravada Buddhism in ancient Cambodia had the result of weakening the semi-divine authority of the Khmer kings, leaving Angkor Wat and other Khmer cities vulnerable to conquest by their Siamese neighbours. Sometimes a city's drive to conquer other cities was the cause of its own defeat. Carthage, weakened by a series of aggressive wars against Rome for commercial and military dominance in the

Mediterranean, was defeated and destroyed in the third war between the two powers.

Though 'peace on Earth' is a frequent prayer today, as in the past, the prevalence of war as a force of destruction and cause of misery for the cities of the world makes it hard to view this hope as a genuine possibility. Perhaps we should remember that those civilizations that were most aggressive were also the most vulnerable to defeat by stronger powers. Ancient Babylon, located 100 km (60 miles) south of Baghdad in Iraq, has been destroyed and rebuilt many times as a result of the rise and fall of militaristic empires – most recently when Iraqi leader Saddam Hussein built a lavish palace over the city's ruins, only to see it fall to American-led forces.

LOSS OF TRADE AND COMMERCE

Trade has always been a city's life-blood, and anything that threatens commerce threatens a city's survival. During the Roman Empire the city of Ephesus on the coast of what is

Right This granite lion was uncovered at Mahabalipuram in south India when the coastline receded following the 2004 tsunami. Dating back to the 7th century, the remains could be part of an ancient port.

now Turkey was an important trading hub. When the city's harbour – its vital link to maritime commerce – began to fill with silt, Roman engineers tried everything they could to save it. They re-engineered the harbour, dredged it and, as a last resort, changed the course of a river. Despite these heroic efforts, the entrance to the sea was pushed to the west and the resulting loss of trade doomed the city.

There were many reasons why ancient cities could lose the trade that sustained them. A rival power could capture control of important trade routes, as happened in Petra in Jordan. Or local trading partners could begin to market their goods directly to foreign buyers, as occurred in Tartessos in Spain. Alternatively, winds and tides could change the position of a spit of land, diverting ships to the settlements further down the coast, as happened in Dunwich in Suffolk, England.

Moreover, as is true today, many ancient cities relied on trade to provide life's necessities. Because of this dependence, when a city's trading partner became weakened by any of the developments already mentioned, its access to vital goods was threatened. Unrest in the Middle East that cuts or slows the flow of oil to the thirsty industrialized countries is a contemporary example of this problem. In addition, friendly cities became enemies (and enemies became friends and trading partners) in the ancient world just as frequently as happens today.

As American philosopher and essayist George Santayana wrote, 'Those who cannot remember the past are condemned to repeat it.' Reflecting on the reasons why cities of the past were lost may help us make the necessary changes to enable our own cities to avoid similar fates.

REDISCOVERY AND RESEARCH

The stories about the rediscovery of lost cities, and the archeological investigations that are helping us to understand how they grew and why they failed, can be just as fascinating as the histories of the cities themselves. During the 18th and 19th centuries intrepid European and American explorers uncovered the ruins of many lost cities around the world. Adventurers hacked their way through the jungle to discover Machu Picchu and crawled through the Taklamakan Desert to explore the oasis cities

Left When the authority of the Khmer kings of ancient Cambodia was weakened by a shift in religious beliefs, the exquisitely carved temples at Angkor fell into ruins and were largely reclaimed by the jungle.

'Those who cannot remember the past are condemned to repeat it.'

of China's Silk Road. Unfortunately the motive behind some expeditions, such as those to Turkey, Greece and Egypt, was collecting antiquities rather than scientific research. However, artefacts now housed in European and American museums provided later researchers with wonderful evidence for study; some of the artefacts are now being returned to museums in their lands of origin.

Currently much of the archeology at the sites of lost cities is being carried out by international teams, many of which include university- or museum-based scholars as well as local researchers. The use of modern technological tools, including images of archeological sites collected from space by satellites, is an exciting recent development that promises many new insights.

A LOOK AHEAD

The cities in this book are presented in six groups. The first four chapters examine lost cities with different geographies – cities that were located on sea coasts, in deserts and on plains, in the hills and mountains, and in the world's jungles and forests. As you will discover, the cities in each of these regions faced a unique set of environmental challenges. The last two chapters examine cities with common themes – those that were ruled by powerful monarchs and those that functioned as sacred religious centres. As the stories of the different cities unfold, the parallels with modern cities that fit into each group become clear and we can start to perceive the lessons for the cities of today in the fate of the lost cities of the past.

Above The eruption of Mount Vesuvius in 79 CE buried Pompeii, near modern Naples, Italy, under tons of ash and debris. The eruption lasted about 19 hours and the column of ash from the volcano was at times 32 km (20 miles) tall.

CHAPTER 1

CITIES OF
THE SEA

Ancient cities on islands or coasts thrived or perished depending on the whims of the sea. When the seas were favourable, trade brought prosperity. But when the forces of wind, waves and water turned foul, sea-coast cities could be inundated in a matter of days. Slower but no less devastating forces of coastal erosion could close harbours, taking away a city's livelihood, or eat away at a city's foundation.

The seas were also ancient highways. Peaceful visitors and pilgrims brought their customs, religions, manuscripts and artefacts with them when they sailed to port cities from distant lands. The journals, letters and sketches of the early travellers provide valuable information for today's researchers.

But the seas also brought travellers with more sinister ambitions. Reports of the rich cities of Meso-America sent home by Spanish explorers paved the way for the Spanish conquest and the fame of port cities on the Mediterranean attracted the attention of powerful empire-builders from Alexander the Great to the Ottoman Turks.

Legendary drowned and underwater cities

The ancient sea-coast cities are among the world's most picturesque and fascinating places. Visitors who approach these cities by water find it easy to imagine them as they once were – thriving sea ports, filled with ships laden with colourful and exotic goods and the sailors, traders and merchants who conducted the business of the city. Because ships often carried foreign travellers (and their philosophies and faiths) in addition to merchandise, sea ports were among the ancient world's most culturally diverse cities.

As their geographical location suggests, water played a key role in the growth and development of sea-coast cities, and often also in their decline and fall. For many, maritime trade was the city's life-blood. When wars, the loss of routes or markets, or damage to the city's harbour interrupted the flow of trade, ports like Tulum in the Mayan Yucatan, Kekova in Turkey and mineral-rich Tartessos in Spain lost their reason for being and soon died. Water from floods, tides, sea-coast storms and tsunamis also brought down thriving cities, including Dwarka in India, Port Royal in Jamaica and the English town of Dunwich in Suffolk.

When a city's ruins lie beneath the waves, water also influences how explorers and archeologists locate and study them. In centuries past, adventurers sailed far from home to explore sites such as Tulum in Mexico and the coastal cities of the kingdom of Lycia in present-day Turkey. More recently, Herakleion in Egypt was discovered when sophisticated underwater scanning devices pinpointed its location. Ironically, the same forces that destroy cities can also reveal their secrets. Fresh details of Mahabalipuram in India were uncovered when the tsunami of 26 December 2004

shifted the shoreline. Perhaps nature will some day reveal the location of sea-coast cities that are still lost, such as Vineta on the Baltic coast and Tartessos in Spain.

The recorded history of actual cities often blends with mythic tales of cities drowned by the gods for their wickedness, or submerged by divine intervention as protection or to teach the inhabitants a lesson. Many lost cities also seem to echo the legends of utopias – paradises of high art and culture lost for ever beneath the sea.

THE CITY OF YS

The legend of the drowned city of Ys has been celebrated in medieval ballads and recounted in folk tales passed down in Brittany's oral tradition. It is said that the city was built by good King Gradlon on land reclaimed from what is now Douarnenez Bay on the north-western coast of France. The city was protected from the waves by a strong dike, though a locked gate could be opened to enable the outflow of tidal water. Only the king had the key.

In the early days of Christianity, Ys was the richest and liveliest trading port on the Atlantic. Luxury goods flowed into the city from far and wide, bringing with them lusty

sailors, temptation and vice. King Gradlon, a pious man who was counselled by St Gwenole, deplored the city's sinfulness and the wayward behaviour of his rebellious daughter Princess Dahut. Though Gwenole foretold the city's fall if its wickedness did not cease, Gradlon was unable to control his subjects or his daughter.

One night, while Gradlon was sleeping, Dahut stole the key and opened the gate to let in her lover. In an instant the ocean rushed in, flooding the city. Grabbing his daughter, Gradlon tried to flee to higher ground on his white horse. As the waves were about to overtake him, St Gwenole commanded the king to throw his wicked daughter into the flood waters. Though he hesitated, Gradlon had no choice but to comply, and escaped to found the city of Quimper. Dahut, it is said, became a mermaid, who put her charms to new use, seducing sailors and fishermen to a watery grave. On calm days, visitors claim to hear the bells of the church of Ys still ringing beneath the bay.

Though the fairytale elements of this story may be specific to Breton and Celtic folklore, in which many similar tales are told, the notion that cities have been drowned as a

Left Mahabalipuram was renowned in ancient times for its carvings. This detail from the Descent of the Ganges shows the Naga Raja (king of the water serpents) and his wife, and the cleft down which water cascaded to simulate the Ganges' descent from heaven.

punishment for wickedness enters the history of many real places. Port Royal in Jamaica, home to pirates who preyed on ships carrying treasures from the Spanish Main, was reputed to be the 'wickedest city on Earth' when a tsunami destroyed it. Similar tales have been told by religious authorities throughout history to encourage virtue. According to medieval Christian legend, the Baltic city of Vineta was drowned because of the sinfulness of its inhabitants.

KITEZH

For other legendary cities, drowning came not as punishment but as divine protection. According to a Russian folk legend, the city of Kitezh was constructed on a beautiful spot on the shore of Lake Svetloyar, north-east of Moscow, by Georgy II, Grand Prince of Vladimir (1189–1238). The legend relates that the people of Kitezh were especially devout and the town was filled with golden-domed churches and monasteries.

In 1237 north-eastern Russia was invaded by the Mongol armies of Batu Khan. Many cities were plundered and burned by the advancing horde. Legend tells that, as the Mongols marched towards Kitezh, Prince Georgy and his soldiers retreated through

Above The highest
building in Tulum, an
important Mayan port
on the Yucatan coast
of Mexico, is called
El Castillo. Torches in
the stone tower, which
served as a lighthouse,
guided trade canoes
through the reef to the
beach below.

the woods and sought refuge in the walled
city. Seeking the easiest route to Kitezh, the
Mongol leader tortured the Russians he had
captured, in order to learn the secret
pathways through the woods. As the Mongol
army approached the town, they were
surprised to see that instead of preparing to
defend themselves, the citizens of Kitezh
were engaged in fervent prayer.

Just as the Mongols began their attack,
fountains of water burst from the ground all
around Kitezh. The attackers fell back and
watched in amazement as the entire town
sank into the lake. The last thing to be seen
of Kitezh was the golden dome of its
cathedral, topped by a cross. Then there
were only waves. Folk beliefs hold that Kitezh
exists to this day, but remains invisible to all
but the pure of heart. Nevertheless, pilgrims
seeking the lake's healing waters often claim
to hear the sound of its bells chiming from
beneath the water.

Though Kitezh may exist only in legend,
many drowned cities with visible ruins are
also sites of pilgrimage. Dwarka in India,
sacred to the Hindu god Krishna, is one such
place. According to Hindu mythology, when
Krishna lived in Dwarka the city flourished,
but when he left for his heavenly abode, the
sea submerged its beautiful buildings in a
matter of moments. It seems that people all
over the world seek to understand the
reasons for floods and other natural
disasters by giving them a divine cause.

PARADISE LOST
The gods can also drown a city to teach its
inhabitants a lesson. Paradise, the stories
seem to say, belongs only to the gods.
Human cities should not be too perfect or
too beautiful. The story of Mahabalipuram is
related in the Hindu epic, the *Mahabharata*.
Mahabalipuram is a real place on the coast
of southern India. According to legend, its

carved temples were so beautiful that the gods became jealous and sent a flood that drowned the city in a single day.

Other paradise cities were lost because perfection led to pride and imperialism. The most famous legendary drowned utopia is, of course, Atlantis. In the original telling, in the Greek philosopher Plato's *Timaeus* and *Critias* (*c.* 360 BCE), Atlantis was not a utopia, but rather the opponent of an imaginary Athens of the distant past that represented the perfect society in Plato's *Republic*. The island city, located by Plato 'beyond the Pillars of Hercules' – today identified with the Straits of Gibraltar – had beauty, sophistication, wealth and power. Though the Atlantean empire encompassed much of the Mediterranean world, its drive for conquest led to an unsuccessful attack on Athens. Soon after the failed invasion, the gods, angered at this hubris, caused Atlantis to sink beneath the waves 'in a single day and night of misfortune'.

The legend of Atlantis has inspired controversy and debate, both in Plato's time and in our own. Is Plato's story history or myth, or a combination of the two? And if Atlantis is a real place, where in the world is it? Over the years the moral lesson of the original Atlantis legend was forgotten. In later retellings Atlantis is more often pictured as a lost paradise – a high civilization that, in some recent esoteric accounts, is powered by crystal energy and filled with spiritually advanced super-beings. Many historical lost cities have been proposed as the location of Atlantis. Akrotiri on the Greek island of Santorini and Tartessos on the Spanish coast are among those that have attracted the attention of contemporary Atlantis hunters.

Above *This 20th-century painting by Ilya Glazunov depicts the drowned city of Kitezh, Russia. Legend says that the city was hidden in Lake Svetloyar to protect it from Mongol invaders.*

'*Many lost cities seem to echo the legends of utopias – paradises of high art and culture lost for ever beneath the sea.*'

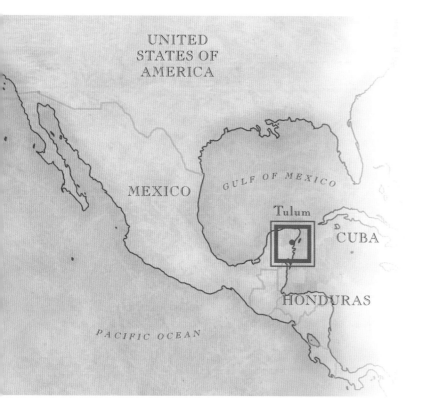

Tulum – city of the dawn

The most sophisticated civilization of pre-Columbian America was the Maya, whose city-states spread throughout Guatemala, the lowland rainforests of Peten in Mexico and the Yucatan Peninsula. Though this civilization was at its peak during the Mayan Classic period (300–800 CE), a few Mayan cities survived into the early 17th century. Among them was Tulum, a small city on the east coast of the Yucatan perched on a cliff above the blue-green waters of the Caribbean Sea.

The name 'Tulum' means 'wall', 'fence' or 'fortification' in Yucatan Mayan. Indeed, Tulum is surrounded by a defensive wall on three sides and on the fourth by the Caribbean. Originally the city may have been called 'Zama', meaning 'city of the dawn or sunrise' – and the rising sun would have been a spectacular sight from the city's high perch above the sea.

TULUM AT ITS HEIGHT

Tulum was most active between 1200 and 1521 CE, when it was probably a busy commercial trading city, joining land and sea-trade routes. Evidence still remains of an early post-Classic-period marketplace in the town. From its port, sea-going canoes carried Yucatan exports such as salt, cacao (chocolate beans), coloured shells, jade and other stones, as well as tropical bird feathers to trading partners in Aztec Mexico, in return for copper tools and ornaments.

Perhaps 500–600 people inhabited the town at its height, living in houses on raised platforms arranged along a street. The town's principal buildings, including the Castillo and the two-storeyed Temple of the

Frescoes, are clustered together near the sea. The murals, which probably decorated the interior and exterior surfaces of the temples, depict classical Mayan gods such as the rain god Chaak and various female divinities performing ceremonies in the bean fields. In

Above This wall painting in the Temple of the Frescoes shows an aged goddess, probably Chak Chel, carrying two images of the rain god Chaak.

Left *The three levels of the Temple of the Frescoes symbolize the three realms of the Mayan universe: the dark underworld inhabited by the dead, the middle level of the human world and the heavenly realm inhabited by the gods.*

another painting Chaak sits mounted on a four-legged animal, which may indicate that the people of Tulum had seen or heard of Spaniards riding on horseback.

TRAVEL IN THE YUCATAN

The first mention of Tulum comes in an account by Spanish explorer Juan Diaz, a member of Juan de Grijalva's expedition that reached the coast of the Yucatan in 1518. He described Tulum as a city so grand that Seville, back in Spain, would not have appeared bigger or better.

American diplomat and lawyer John L. Stephens and English topographical artist Frederick Catherwood visited the site in 1842. Their book, *Incidents of Travel in Yucatan,* which combined Stephens' text with Catherwood's magnificent illustrations, is credited with bringing the Mayan culture back into the minds of the Western world.

Today Tulum is a popular destination for tourists, as it lies just 120 km (75 miles) south of the beach resort of Cancun. Visitors are drawn to the site by its picturesque setting on the scenic Caribbean coastline.

WHY WAS TULUM ABANDONED?

When Spanish explorers arrived in the Yucatan in the early 16th century, the greatness of the Mayan civilization was already in eclipse. The Classic-period cities of Copán (see pages 94–95), Tikal (see pages 98–99) and Palenque (see pages 100–101) had already been abandoned, perhaps because of over-exploitation of the fragile soils of the rainforest environment.

After the collapse, the culture of surviving Mayan cities like Tulum became mixed with other influences, such as the Toltec culture from central Mexico and the Mixtec culture from the hilly country of Oaxaca. Between

1200 and 1540 CE numerous wars erupted between Yucatan city-states under Toltec influence and those ruled by the Maya, each jealous of the power and lands of the other.

The arrival of the Spanish completed the collapse of the Maya. Spanish conquistadors used Mayan cities for their settlements, and Mayan ruins were often buried under layers of new colonial construction.

Tulum, protected by defensive walls and dense forests, probably survived for a while beyond the Spanish conquest, perhaps because of its geographical location. The great majority of late Mayan trade and commerce took place by sea, since the roads were poor and cargoes heavy. This meant that, as a well-positioned port and trade hub, Tulum was able to continue well past the general Mayan decline. archeologists estimate that it was finally abandoned around the end of the 16th century.

'Tulum was a city so grand that even Seville, back in Spain, would not have appeared bigger or better.'

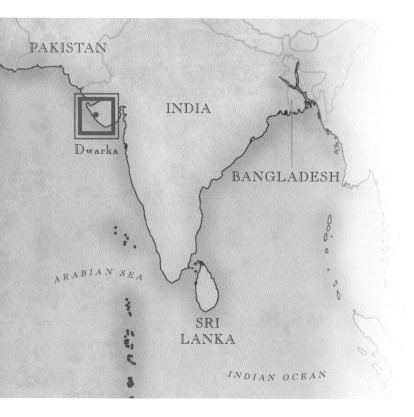

Dwarka – Krishna's holy city

Dwarka, on the extreme western tip of the Kathiawar Peninsula in Gujarat, India, is one of the four most holy Hindu pilgrimage sites. Sacred to the Hindu god Krishna, who is said to have founded and settled in the city, Dwarka is mentioned in the Hindu national epic, the Mahabharata, *and in other Hindu scriptures.*

Recent archeological discoveries under the sea support a long history for the site, dating back to perhaps 2000 BCE.

LEGENDARY DWARKA

The Hindu epic, the *Mahabharata*, describes Dwarka's founding by Krishna on 12 parcels of land reclaimed from the sea. The text paints a vivid picture of life in the ancient city. When Krishna dwelled there, Dwarka was filled with many beautiful gardens, ponds and palaces. The men and women who lived in the city of Dwarka decorated themselves with jewels, ornaments, scents and sandals. Traders brought merchandise to marketplaces that had been cleanly swept and sprinkled with water. Noble people, conveyed in chariots and carriages or mounted on horses and elephants, came to pay their respects, and entertainers and

poets amused the god by dancing, singing and playing on musical instruments. Religion flourished, too. Brahmin priests read the Vedas (Hindu scriptures), and holy and virtuous men sang praises eight times each day.

After Krishna left the city for his heavenly abode, Dwarka was inundated, ushering in the current dark age, known as the Kali Yuga. As the charioteer Arjuna describes the event in the *Mahabharata*, the sea broke its boundary and rushed into the city, submerging the beautiful buildings one by one. In a matter of moments, it was all over – there was no trace of the city; Dwarka was just a memory.

WHY DWARKA DROWNED

Experience of the devastation caused by the tsunami of 26 December 2004 has fuelled

speculation that a similar cataclysmic event could possibly have caused Dwarka's destruction. Some scientists have wondered whether a tsunami might have struck the coast of Gujarat in around 1500 BCE, drowning the ancient city.

However, it is likely that Dwarka's destruction has a less dramatic explanation. Severe coastal erosion at the rate of 4 metres (13 feet) per year has been established as the primary reason for the city's decline. Natural and human-created coastal erosion is a prevalent and costly problem worldwide. Poorly designed coastal development, damage caused by storms and flooding, and continued global warming accompanied by rising sea levels have resulted in a marked increase in the land lost to coastal erosion around the world. If sea levels were to rise by just 5.5–6 metres (18–20 feet), scientists estimate that as many as 60 million people in India and Bangladesh would be displaced.

RECENT ARCHEOLOGICAL FINDS

The search for the lost city of Dwarka has been going on since the 1930s. Between 1997 and 2001, the Marine archeological

'In a matter of moments, it was all over – there was no trace of the city; Dwarka was just a memory.'

Centre of India's National Institute of Oceanography took part in the exploration. Marine archeologists making use of scuba equipment, Global Positioning System data and underwater still and video cameras managed to identify a large number of stone structures beneath the water, including the remains of an ancient jetty and more than 120 stone anchors of various types. These finds are an indication that Dwarka had been an important port since at least the early historical period of Indian history (2500–1500 BCE).

DWARKA TODAY

Seldom visited by Westerners because of its remote location, Dwarka thrives today as a Hindu pilgrimage site. In the 7th century the Hindu sage Shankaracharya established four Divine Abodes or *dhamas* in each of the cardinal points of the country, with Dwarka as the abode of the west. Dwarka is also one of India's Seven Sacred Cities, which means that people who die within its boundaries are said to achieve *moksha*, or permanent liberation from suffering. Though Dwarka's original temples were destroyed during the 11th to 15th centuries by Muslim armies, they have repeatedly been rebuilt. The current temple Jagatmandir, also known as Sri Dwarkadish, was rebuilt in 1730.

Today Dwarka is also visited by pilgrims because of its association with the beloved Hindu saint Mira Bai. In the 16th century, Mira Bai renounced her splendid and luxurious life as the wife of a powerful king to dedicate herself to the worship of Krishna. According to legend, when Mira Bai lived in Dwarka during the last years of her life, her powerful devotion caused Krishna to manifest physically in order to eat, sing, dance and play with her.

Above Dwarka's Jagatmandir Temple, built in 1730, stands 52 metres (170 feet) tall. The temple's five storeys are supported by 72 pillars, a number with astrological significance found in sacred architecture around the world.

Akrotiri – Bronze Age Aegean port

A favourite stop on the tourist track through the Greek Islands of the Aegean Sea is Santorini (Thera in Greek). Its blinding white, cube-shaped villages hug the tops of sheer west-facing cliffs. The geography of Santorini testifies to its violent past. Most of the terrain, including the black sand beaches, is covered by volcanic debris, a reminder of the cataclysm that gave the island its shape.

The cliffs to which the villages cling are actually the lip of the caldera (basin-shaped crater) of an ancient volcano. Its eruption in about 1500 BCE buried the island and its original seaside town of Akrotiri under tons of pumice and ash.

ANCIENT AKROTIRI

The bustling port town of Akrotiri on the island's fertile eastern plain came to prominence during the late Bronze Age (*c.* 2000–1550 BCE). The town's elaborate drainage system, with pipes to carry both hot and cold water, and sophisticated multi-storey buildings, wall paintings, furniture and artefacts indicate great cultural development and a life of grace, ease and prosperity. Trading ships from Minoan Crete and mainland Greece, as well as from ports in Cyprus, Syria and Egypt, connected the island with other high civilizations.

Akrotiri's lovely wall paintings create a vivid portrait of life in the ancient city. A mural of Thera's landscape in springtime shows crocuses blooming among the rocks, above which swallows fly to their nests bearing food for their open-mouthed chicks.

In another painting two young fishermen proudly hold up strings of fish, their day's catch. Two children with boxing gloves on their right hands are captured on another wall in the midst of their play.

The wall paintings also depict the town's spiritual life, which centred on worship of the Great Goddess. A painting shows three women gathering crocuses in a rocky landscape and offering them to a seated female figure. The girls are dressed in the style of a priestess from the Crete of King Minos, with flounced skirts and open bodices. The seated woman has flowing black hair and intricate goddess-like clothing and jewellery. On the door jamb of another room, a young woman, wearing a long heavy robe, carries a brazier with glowing charcoal, sprinkling it with incense, which she may be carrying from room to room.

THE CITY'S VIOLENT END

All this grace and beauty came to an abrupt end when a series of violent earthquakes shook the island, causing extensive damage. Then, some months or years later, in about 1500 BCE, Thera's volcano erupted. Ash and

debris covered the town completely, preserving and protecting the buildings and their contents. After blasting out its molten interior, Thera's volcano collapsed, leaving the crescent-shaped island that exists today.

Archeologists have vigorously debated the sequence of events that led to the collapse of Akrotiri. Some believe that extensive repairs, including the demolition of earthquake-weakened structures and a programme of restoration and rebuilding, were under way at the time of the eruption. It seems that ancient people were as prone as we are to rebuilding their homes in places that have proved geologically dangerous. However, unlike many towns along the Gulf of Mexico in the years before Hurricane Katrina, Akrotiri had a well-conceived evacuation plan. The absence of bodies preserved in the ashes, and of jewellery and other small valuables, indicates that residents heeded the signs pointing to an impending eruption and fled to safety.

DISCOVERY AND EXCAVATION

The first supporting evidence for the existence of Akrotiri came to light towards

Right *This famous wall painting, showing two youths boxing, was uncovered on the first floor of one of the most important buildings of ancient Akrotiri. Frescoes like these paint a charming picture of the city's daily life.*

the end of the 19th century. Systematic excavations were commenced in 1967, when Professor Spyridon Marinatos of the archeological Society of Athens started to explore Akrotiri in the hope of proving his theory that the eruption of Thera's volcano had been responsible for the collapse of the Minoan civilization on Crete. Since the death of Professor Marinatos in 1974, excavations at Akrotiri have been continued under the direction of Professor Christos Doumas.

Current thinking is that the eruption of Thera's volcano could not have damaged towns on Crete directly, as they lie 112 km (70 miles) away. However, huge tsunamis probably rolled outwards from the blast, and Crete lay in their path. Perhaps these waves link Thera with Plato's tale of Atlantis – another beautiful, civilized island that vanished suddenly and mysteriously beneath the waves.

Today, the superb wall paintings have been removed to a special gallery at the National archeological Museum in Athens, and the archeological site, covered by a protective canopy, is open to the public.

Vineta – city of the 12 gates

Vineta is an ancient (or possibly legendary) port city on the German or Polish coast of the Baltic Sea. The earliest written account of the city is by Arabic writer Ibrahim ibn Yaqub, who visited the area as an envoy of the Caliph of Cordoba around 970 CE. He described it as a large city built in the marshes near the sea in the far north-west of the country of Misiko (Poland), with 12 gates and a powerful army to protect it.

Right *This 9th-century Viking helmet, made of iron, is one of the artefacts on display in the Viking Ship Museum in Oslo, Norway. It is likely that the Jomsviking brothers of Vineta wore similar fighting gear.*

Traders in the 11th and 12th centuries described Vineta as the most powerful trading city on the Baltic coast.

VIKING AGE VINETA

The Nordic name for Vineta is *Jumme, Jumneta* or *Jomsberg*. Icelandic sagas of the 12th and 13th centuries describe Jomsberg as an important Viking trading city dating back to 500 CE, with links to Russia, Greece and Phoenicia.

According to the Jomsvikinga Saga (*c.* 1240 CE), Jomsberg was founded by a guild of mercenary soldiers and traders called the Jomsvikings. Staunchly pagan, they were dedicated to the worship of Norse deities such as Odin and Thor. Membership of the Jomsvikings was restricted to men of proven valour, who agreed to be governed by a strict code of moral conduct. To gain admission to the brotherhood, candidates needed to prove their courage in a ritual dual or other feat of strength. Jomsvikings pledged to defend each other to the death and were forbidden to quarrel or speak ill of each other or to show fear in the face of an enemy. All spoils of battle – and, some say,

Left *Narrow longboats packed with warriors, like these dragon boats from the 10th or 11th century, helped make the Vikings the dominant sea power in northern Europe for three centuries from about 800 CE.*

of their piracy on the high seas – were distributed equally among the brotherhood. Like the crusading orders of knights of medieval Europe, the Jomsvikings ventured out to fight on behalf of any lord able to pay their substantial fees.

The historian Saxo Grammaticus (c. 1200 CE) wrote in his history of Denmark that in around 980 CE the Danish King Harald Bluetooth fled from a rebellion led by his son, Sweyn Forkbeard, to a fortress at Jomsberg. Some accounts credit Harald Bluetooth with founding the Jomsvikings, teaching them seafaring skills and leading them on pirate raids against his enemies from the north. It is said that, at its height, the harbour at Jomsberg held 30–300 ships.

HISTORICAL VINETA
According to historical accounts, control of Vineta or Jomsberg changed hands several times during the Middle Ages. Between 980 and 1150 CE the Jomsvikings battled kings from Sweden, Denmark and Norway. In one key battle, the brotherhood joined forces with the enemies of King Olaf of Sweden to annihilate his fleet and delay the

Christianizing of Scandinavia, which was supported by Olaf.

Several key defeats caused the power of the Jomsvikings to wane. In 1043 King Magnus I of Norway sacked Jomsberg, destroyed its fortress and put the surviving members of the brotherhood to death. Later, the Danish kings Niels (d. 1134) and Valdemar the Great (d. 1182) are said to have drowned the city of Vineta by opening the dikes that held back the waters of the River Oder.

According to medieval Christian legend, the city sank in a storm tide during the late Middle Ages, drowned because of the sinfulness of its inhabitants. However, it is more likely that Vineta sank because of a natural or human-caused shift in the water-distribution channels in the delta of the River Oder.

VINETA TODAY
Although archeologists have searched for the remains of the city, and several contemporary cities in Poland and Germany claim to be built on its site, Vineta remains lost to this day.

The most likely site for Vineta is the trading city of Wolin in north-western Poland. Excavations there revealed the remains of a large international trading city from the Viking Age and early Middle Ages. Each August Wolin holds a Jomsberg-Vineta festival featuring races between replicas of Viking and Slavic ships, mock battles, historical costumes, archery tournaments and medieval crafts. The German towns of Zinnowitz on Usedom Island and Barth in Western Pomerania, on a lagoon of the Baltic Sea, also claim to be the site of Vineta. Both these cities have summer festivals with dance, music and theatrical performances.

'Traders in the 11th and 12th centuries described Vineta as the most powerful trading city on the Baltic coast.'

Kekova, Simena and Teimiussa – Lycia's sea-coast cities

Lycia was a tightly knit confederation of independent city-states with a history dating back to at least 1250 BCE. It occupied a mountainous and densely forested region along the south-western coast of Turkey.

Opposite This chest-type tomb lies half-submerged in shallow waters off the coast of Kekova, Turkey. The tombs were important in the Lycian cult of ancestor worship.

Today, the partially submerged ruins of Lycia's ancient seaside cities – Kekova, Simena and Teimiussa – can be viewed from a boat travelling along Turkey's sunny Mediterranean coast.

LYCIA'S SEA-COAST RUINS

Along the edge of Turkey's Kekova Island lie the submerged ruins of the buildings and walls of an ancient city. archeologists believe that this city is a Lycian sea port from which maritime trade was conducted with other Lycian towns and with various parts of the Greek world. Because of the threat of piracy, the port was probably heavily fortified and served both as a refuge in times of peril and as an early warning post of danger heading to the Lycian mainland.

Along the mainland coastline, across from Kekova, are the chest-like sarcophagus tombs of an ancient necropolis, near the ruins of the ancient Lycian city of Teimiussa. The bay of Teimiussa, surrounded by green hills, made an excellent harbour for Lycian ships. Further down the coast are the ruins of ancient Simena, which lie below the crenellated ramparts of a ruined hilltop

castle, held by the Romans and later by the Byzantine Empire. Inside the castle is a small rock-cut theatre, used during Roman times. A lone Lycian sarcophagus stands in shallow water below the town.

Over the centuries Lycia's strategically important location made it a tempting conquest for a succession of Mediterranean powers: Persia, Greece, the Macedonian armies of Alexander the Great, the Roman Empire, the Byzantine Empire and finally the Ottoman (Turkish) Empire. Lycia also suffered from natural disasters, such as a devastating earthquake in the 2nd century that partially sank the sea port on Kekova Island. Rebuilt and still flourishing during the Byzantine Empire, the port was abandoned by the end of the 8th century because of pirate attacks and Arab raids. The Lycian coast was not cleared of piracy until the British Navy began patrolling the area during the 18th and 19th centuries.

DISCOVERY OF LYCIA

The best-known early explorer of Lycia was British adventurer Sir Charles Fellows, whose work is credited with bringing Lycia to the

attention of the West. The son of a wealthy silk merchant and banker, Fellows organized his first expedition to Lycia in 1838. On this and subsequent trips he discovered the location of Xanthos, Lycia's capital and most famous city, as well as the remains of 13 other Lycian cities. In many cases Fellows was the first Westerner to see the city since it had been abandoned in late antiquity.

After returning to England, Fellows published an account of his explorations, which inspired the British Museum to send a naval vessel to Lycia to collect pieces of its art for conservation. During the 1850s the exhibition of these pieces in London caused a sensation almost as great as the exhibiting of the Elgin Marbles from the Greek Parthenon 40 years earlier.

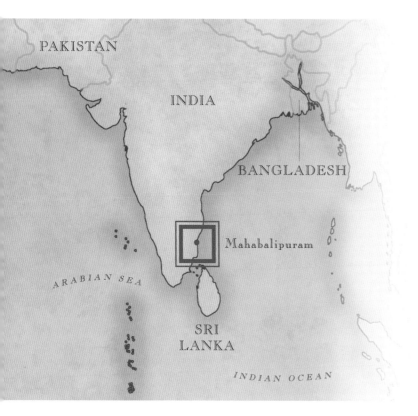

Mahabalipuram – city of the seven pagodas

When the destructive tsunami of 26 December 2004 receded, it revealed previously hidden details of the underwater ruins of Mahabalipuram, the ancient port city of the Pallava dynasty kings who ruled the Indian state of Tamil Nadu from the 4th to 9th centuries. The ruins are probably part of the City of the Seven Pagodas, long thought to be a fanciful 'traveller's tale'.

First discovered in 2002 by divers from India and England, the underwater ruins of Mahabalipuram are a significant addition to the wonders of a lost city of extraordinary beauty and significance.

SEVEN FABULOUS TEMPLES

During the reign of the great Pallava king Narasimhavaraman I (*c.* 630–670 CE), the city of Mahabalipuram was a flourishing sea port. From its harbour the king sent a fleet of ships to conquer Sri Lanka and place a king loyal to the Pallavas on its throne. Narasimhavaraman and his successor Pallava kings embellished their port city with exquisitely carved temples cut from huge granite boulders, lavish cave-temples sculpted from rock monoliths and bas-relief sculptures depicting mythic stories, images of the gods and scenes from Indian village life in the 7th century. The city was adorned with more than 100 intricate pieces of sculpture, which are admired today as the finest expression of Indian rock-cut and sculpted art.

The City of the Seven Pagodas was first described by the astronomer, engineer and explorer John Goldingham, who visited the site in 1798. He recorded the myth of a large city that once stood on the coast. It was so beautiful that the gods became jealous and sent a flood that swallowed the city in a single day. According to the myth, the city had seven fabulous temples, six of which were submerged in the flood. The seventh is still standing on the coast. Known today as the Shore Temple, it is visited frequently by pilgrims and tourists. Recent excavations at the site have revealed that the Shore Temple was itself washed away, probably by a cyclone, and was reconstructed some time later, stone by stone, from the sea.

THE FLOOD MYTH

Perhaps the most interesting feature of the Mahabalipuram carvings is the depiction of a flood myth with similarities to the story of Noah in the Bible. According to the Indian version, the sage Bhagiratha brought down the River Ganges from heaven to purify the souls of his ancestors. When he realized that the flood would drown the Earth, he did penance and prayed to the god Shiva to intervene. Shiva came down to Earth and let the deluge trickle through his hair, dividing it safely into the streams that flow all over the world. This strange sight caused all the animals of the world to gather around Shiva in wonder and amazement.

This ancient story is an eerie parallel to the 2004 tsunami, which battered the ruins of Mahabalipuram. Scientists studying the site are investigating various possible reasons for the historical drowning of the city, including sea-level fluctuations, coastal erosion and earthquakes causing shoreline changes. If, as some researchers believe, the city was originally submerged following the last Ice Age, the settlement is more than 5,000 years old, dating back to about 3000 BCE – the approximate date given for the biblical flood.

REDISCOVERY

The underwater ruins of Mahabalipuram were first discovered by a joint team composed of divers from the Indian National Institute of Oceanography and the Scientific Exploration Society, which is based in Dorset in the UK. In their first expedition to the site in April 2002, divers located the

Right The enormous Arjuna's Penance, also known as the Descent of the Ganges, was carved in the mid-7th century from two monumental boulders. It measures 30 metres (96 feet) long by 13 metres (43 feet) high.

remains of walls and rectangular stone building blocks in 5–8 metres (15–25 feet) of water, less than 500–700 metres (½ mile) from the Shore Temple. The underwater site was found to be very large, and divers were able to explore only a small portion.

The receding wave of the 2004 tsunami removed sand deposits and exposed more details of the underwater city. The most significant new discovery is a bas-relief that appears to be part of a temple wall and includes the elaborately carved head of an elephant and a flying horse. Above the elephant's head is a rock niche with the carved statue of a god. Near by, the tsunami revealed the sculpture of a reclining lion. It is likely that more evidence of the fabled City of the Seven Pagodas awaits discovery.

'The city was adorned with more than 100 intricate pieces of sculpture, which are admired today as the finest expression of Indian rock-cut and sculpted art.'

Mahabalipuram

Ancient Mahabalipuram was a city of wonders. Its cave-temples, chariot-shrines carved from rock monoliths, sculpted bas-reliefs and structural temples, built between the 7th and 9th centuries, are among the world's most beautiful and dramatic sacred monuments.

Today, tourists and pilgrims flock to visit the sites, including the famous Arjuna's Penance. This huge bas-relief is carved from two rocks separated by a cleft down which water may have been poured to simulate a waterfall. On one side a carved figure raises his arms in a yoga posture in front of the god Shiva. On the other side are many carvings of people and animals, including life-size elephants. The bas-relief may tell the story from the *Mahabharata* in which Arjuna does penance to obtain Shiva's weapon and thus the god's power. Alternatively, the yoga figure may represent the sage Bhagiratha, who also did penance to win Shiva's help after calling down the flood waters of the Ganges.

Near the shrine of the elephant-headed god Ganesh, there is a huge boulder known as Krishna's Butterball. Legend says several of the Pallava kings tried to move the stone, but neither kings nor elephants could change its position by even a fraction.

The Shore Temple, built in the early 8th century, is the earliest-known example of a free-standing Indian temple constructed of granite blocks. Its elaborately decorated pyramid towers, one facing east and one west, honour Shiva. Inside the larger tower is a 16-sided, polished Shiva lingam, symbolizing his powers of creation and destruction. Between the two towers is a rectangular shrine to Vishnu. There are many other shrines within the complex, as well as a circumambulation pathway and other elements influenced by Buddhist design style.

① PANCHA RATHAS

These five shrines were carved in the 7th century during the reign of King Narasimhavaraman I. Each temple is a monolith, carved whole from an outcrop of living rock. The name Pancha Rathas means 'five chariots' and each of the chariots has been named for the Pandava brothers (Arjuna, Bhima, Yudhishtra, Nakula and Sahadeva) and their wife, Draupadi. They are all characters who feature in the *Mahabharata*. The structure of the *rathas* combines the earlier tradition of cave-temples with the later style of free-standing structures like the Shore Temple. The carving of each *ratha* imitates in stone the wooden timber supports, beams and brackets of free-standing stone construction. Each *ratha* is sculpted in a different style.

② NAKULA SAHADEVA RATHA

The barrel-vaulted roof of this shrine links it with the rock-carved elephant standing next to it. The technical name for this roof shape is *gajaprstika*, which literally means 'an elephant's backside'. The rear end of the shrine lines up with that of the rock elephant, indicating that the shrine is dedicated to Indra, the Hindu god of thunder and war. Indra is known to smash the cities of his enemies with the rage of a wild elephant, as well as bringing thunderclouds of violent but refreshing rain.

③ ANIMAL SCULPTURES

In addition to Indra's elephant, life-size sculptures of other mythological animals stand near the *rathas*. A carving of Nandi, the bull that is the mount of the Hindu god Shiva, kneels behind the Arjuna Ratha. The carved lion may be an emblem of the Pallava dynasty kings who built the shrines. Animal sculptures like these adorn many of Mahabalipuram's walls and temples. A granite statue of a reclining lion and a half-completed rock relief of an elephant were among the treasures revealed after the coastline receded near the Shore Temple following the tsunami of 2004. They may be part of a submerged temple that has been covered with sand for centuries.

④ DRAUPADI RATHA

The smallest and simplest of the *rathas*, this shrine is dedicated to the Hindu goddess Durga, a warrior form of the supreme goddess Devi. The shrine is shaped to resemble a hut with a thatched roof. Guarding the doorway are two carved *shalabhanjikas*, fertility figures linked to Durga in her aspect of embodying feminine and creative energy. Inside the *ratha* is a carving of Durga with a devotee preparing to cut off his own head as a sacrifice to the goddess.

⑤ ARJUNA RATHA

This shrine resembles a miniature palace, complete with sculpted pilasters (decorative columns that project only slightly from the wall), miniature roof shrines and an octagonal dome. The central sculpture of the Arjuna Ratha shows Shiva, the cosmic dancer and destroyer god in Hindu mythology, with his legs crossed, leaning on his mount Nandi.

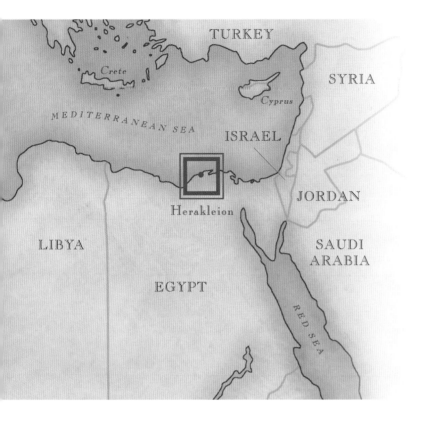

Herakleion – Egypt's sunken treasures

Beneath the surface of the Mediterranean, 6.5 km (4 miles) offshore in Egypt's Aboukir Bay, underwater archeologists have found the fabulous remains of the ancient city of Herakleion. Once strategically located at the mouth of a branch of the Nile River, Herakleion was Egypt's main port in the time of the late pharaohs.

Almost untouched by time, the ruins have already yielded many sunken treasures, including colossal statues, tablets with hieroglyphic writing and a trove of gold coins and ancient jewellery.

PORT CITY OF THE PHARAOHS

The history of the Nile Delta region dates back thousands of years, to the time when Egypt's ports harboured ships carrying goods from Crete, Phoenicia and the islands of the Aegean Sea. The Greek historian Herodotus (484–c. 425 BCE) wrote a vivid description of the great cities of the Nile Delta, which he visited in 450 BCE.

Prominent among these great cities, as archeologists now believe, was Herakleion, once a thriving centre of both business and religion. Though trade was the city's life-blood, among the underwater finds is a temple dedicated to the Greek and Roman hero-god Herakles (Hercules), who was also venerated in Egypt. According to legend, Herakleion was also a city of love. In Homer's account of the Trojan War, the city was the refuge to which the beautiful Helen and her lover Paris, Prince of Troy, fled to

escape Helen's jealous husband Menelaus. Near by, in Alexandria's eastern harbour, divers have discovered the submerged royal quarters of Antirhodos Island, where Egyptian Queen Cleopatra VII (69–30 BCE) had a palace. Cleopatra's stormy love affairs with Roman emperor Julius Caesar and his military commander Mark Antony once rocked the ancient world.

Records show that Herakleion was a wealthy city whose riches came from taxes levied on its merchants and traders. Although the commerce was said to have led to relaxed civic morals, the city was also a place of pilgrimage for people from all over the eastern Mediterranean.

Herakleion's importance as a trading hub declined after the foundation of the port city Alexandria in the 4th century BCE. Over the centuries, it was ruled by the Pharaonic, Ptolemaic, Roman and Byzantine Empires. The recovery of a colossal statue of Hapi, an Egyptian god of fertility, and a statue of a Ptolemaic queen dressed as the Egyptian goddess Isis indicate the city's religious importance. Other significant finds include hieroglyphic stone tablets and a black granite

slab inscribed with an edict from Pharaoh Nektanebos I (378–362 BC) that imposed a 10 per cent tax on Greek goods, payable to the temple of the Pharaonic goddess Neith.

DISCOVERY OF HERAKLEION

Until quite recently historians knew of Herakleion from Greek accounts, but no one had seen the evidence. In 1961 amateur Egyptian diver Kamel Abul-Saadat succeeded in locating remarkable treasures in Alexandria's eastern harbour. His reports sparked a UNESCO-sponsored survey mission in 1968, which confirmed his finds.

Then in 1992 a team of divers from the Paris-based European Institute for Underwater Archaeology, led by marine archeologist Franck Goddio, began to survey and map the eastern harbour of Alexandria and nearby Aboukir Bay using the latest technology, including side-scan sonar, magnetometers, sub-bottom profiling and satellite-assisted Global Positioning System data. In 2000 Goddio and his team announced that they had pinpointed the location of Herakleion, and exhibited the first of its stunning archeological treasures.

WHAT HAPPENED TO HERAKLEION?

Scientists have proposed several theories to account for the city's destruction. Some speculate that earthquakes and tsunamis drowned the city some 1,300 years ago. Others say that the city collapsed because of hydrographic and geological changes, including floods, alterations in sea level and other subsidence factors. Coastal cities around the world are vulnerable to similar disasters.

Egyptian officials are currently working to clean up the waters of Alexandria Bay. Although sediment in the water makes the underwater artefacts difficult to see, the blanket of sediment has actually served to protect the relics from seawater erosion. Ambitious plans for the area, once the waters are clear, include allowing divers to visit the sites and building the world's first underwater museum so that tourists can see for themselves the remains of this Pharaonic city beneath the waves.

Left This statue of Hapi, an Egyptian god of fertility and the inundation of the Nile, is among the important finds made by the international team under the leadership of French archeologist, Franck Goddio.

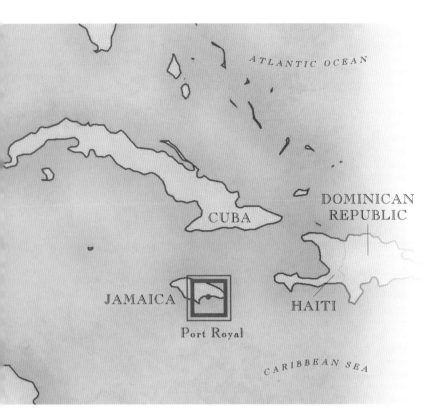

ATLANTIC OCEAN

CUBA

DOMINICAN
REPUBLIC

JAMAICA

HAITI

Port Royal

CARIBBEAN SEA

Port Royal – Caribbean pirate haven

On the southern coast of Jamaica, just south of Cuba, is the sunken city of Port Royal. Founded by the British, who won control of Jamaica from the Spanish in 1655, Port Royal was one of the largest towns in the English colonies of the New World during the late 17th century.

Port Royal was especially notorious as a haven for the pirates and privateers who plundered ships carrying gold, silver, gems, spices, hardwoods and other treasures from the Spanish Main as they passed through the Caribbean on their way to Spain.

THE 'WICKEDEST CITY ON EARTH'

In 1654 England's Lord Protector, Oliver Cromwell, ordered his navy to attack the Spanish-held island of Hispaniola, which lies between Cuba and Puerto Rico. The British attackers were defeated by the Spanish defenders, who had been forewarned. On their retreat, the British fleet captured the poorly protected island of Jamaica.

After the restoration of the British monarchy, the small town located on the spit of sand separating Kingston Harbour from the Caribbean was renamed Port Royal. Because of its strategic location protecting a deep-water harbour where as many as 500 ships could easily be loaded and unloaded, the town grew quickly. Between 1660 and 1692 it was the most economically important British port in the New World.

Much of Port Royal's wealth was generated by its pirates and privateers. Pirates first came to Port Royal from nearby Tortuga, invited by the British to help defend the town from Spanish attack. After peace with Spain in 1660, these same buccaneers obtained letters of marque from British authorities giving them permission to raid and capture merchant ships sailing from the Spanish Main (the Caribbean coast of Spanish colonies in Central and South

Left In this 17th-century engraving, privateers led by Henry Morgan, captain of Port Royal's Volunteer Regiment, defeat the Spanish forces of Vice Admiral Alonso del Campo y Espinosa at the Battle of Maracaibo Bar in 1669.

'Port Royal was home to merchants, artisans and ship captains, as well as the notorious pirates and privateers who gave the city its reputation as the wickedest city on Earth.'

America). Historians estimate that by 1689 nearly half of Port Royal's 6,500–7,000 inhabitants were involved in privateering, or legal piracy. Port Royal also did a thriving business in the trade of slaves, sugar and raw materials from the New World.

Historians calculate that, at its height, the town covered 20 hectares (51 acres) and had more than 2,000 buildings made of brick and timber, some four storeys tall. It was home to merchants, artisans and ship captains, as well as the notorious pirates and privateers who gave the city its reputation as the wickedest city on Earth. Early records show that the authorities were tolerant of prostitution, gambling and other vices. However, they also permitted religious diversity: Quaker, Catholic, Puritan and Jewish merchants, as well as followers of the Church of England, lived and practised in peaceful coexistence.

DESTRUCTION

On 7 June 1692, shortly before noon, a massive earthquake rocked Port Royal. As a result of the quake and the tsunamis that followed, about two-thirds of the city collapsed into rubble or sank into Kingston Harbour. Historians estimate that 2,000 people perished instantly and that an additional 3,000 died in the following days from injuries and disease. The exact time when the quake took place is recorded on a pocket watch, made in France in about 1686, which was recovered during an archeological excavation in 1960. The watch's hands are frozen at 11.43 a.m.

Though an attempt was made to rebuild the city, Port Royal was destroyed again by a massive fire in 1703. Following a severe storm and two earthquakes in 1722, the town disappeared for the last time. Once called the Sodom of the New World, Port Royal experienced a final destruction that seems little short of biblical.

ARCHEOLOGICAL INVESTIGATION

From 1981 to 1990 the underwater ruins of Port Royal were investigated by teams from the Institute of Nautical Archaeology of Texas A&M University, in cooperation with the Jamaica National Heritage Trust. The cultural features and archeological context of Port Royal's ruins have been preserved, despite the passage of time. Many of the streets in the centre of town did not collapse, but simply sank vertically into Kingston Bay, providing us with a unique window into the past.

Underwater archeologists have been able to study the remains of several houses on Lime Street in the town's commercial centre. From the eight buildings explored, they have recovered artefacts that provide us with fascinating information about daily life during the 17th century. The discoveries include porcelain and pewter cups and bowls, forks, spoons and candlesticks, and gold and pearl jewellery.

Today, Port Royal is an isolated fishing village at the end of a long spit of sand. Plans are underway to develop the village into a tourist destination serviced by cruise ships, with the town's archeological heritage as the featured attraction. An underwater museum-aquarium, for example, will allow visitors to view tropical sea life and explore the town's colourful past.

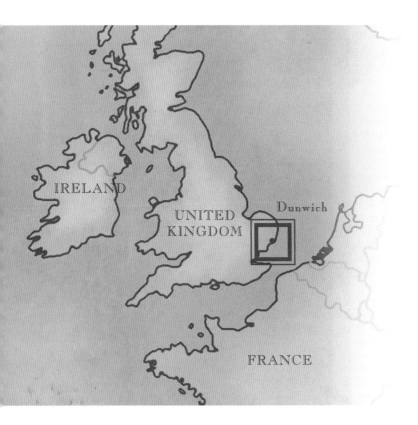

Dunwich – Suffolk's medieval port

In the early Middle Ages, Dunwich was a large town with a thriving sea port in Suffolk on the east coast of England. It was noted as the centre of the English wool trade and for its many churches, including Greyfriars, a Franciscan priory founded in c. 1228.

Right *The ruins of Greyfriars, a Franciscan priory founded by Richard FitzJohn in the 13th century, now stand only a short distance from the eroding cliffs. The ruins will soon be lost to the sea.*

Beginning in 1287 and continuing to this day, almost the entire town has fallen into the sea. The collapse of Dunwich is a visible contemporary example of how a city can be lost.

HISTORICAL DUNWICH

Dunwich dates back to Saxon times, and by the turn of the 1st millennium the town was prosperous and growing. The Domesday Book, a survey of England completed in 1086 for William the Conqueror, records that Dunwich had three churches and about 3,000 inhabitants.

At its height, during the 12th and 13th centuries, Dunwich was a centre of religious and maritime power, with at least eight churches and five houses of religious orders, including Greyfriars and Blackfriars, a Dominican priory. It also had two hospitals, including one for people with leprosy.

The town's location on a splendid natural harbour at the mouth of the River Blythe encouraged fishing and maritime trade. Merchant ships exported wool and grain and brought back fur and timber from Iceland and the Baltic region, cloth from the Netherlands and wine from France. An exceptionally low tide in October 2005 uncovered timbers and piles driven into the seabed. Probably part of a medieval shipyard slipway, these remains support the theory that Dunwich had a busy ship-building industry. Military ships also sailed from Dunwich, including 30 in the fleet that King Henry III sent to war against France in 1230.

Dunwich's favourable location enabled another kind of prosperity. Ships leaving the villages of Southwold, Walberswick and Blythburgh to the north had to sail past Dunwich to reach the sea. Dunwich claimed the right to collect tolls from every ship that passed and, at times, insisted that every incoming ship unload at its port and sell its goods in the Dunwich town market.

DECLINE AND FALL

Ironically the location of Dunwich also led to its decline and fall. In 1286–1288 great storms flooded the town and accelerated the shift of a sandy spit of land called Kings Holme, partially blocking the opening to Dunwich harbour. Another storm in 1328 and an even more violent storm in 1342

further eroded the cliffs on the east side of Dunwich, causing 400 houses and several churches to fall into the sea.

Equally devastating to the people of Dunwich was the fact that the storms diverted the flow of the River Blythe. The river cut a new channel to the sea 1.6 km (1 mile) to the north, near the village of Walberswick. Dismayed at the loss of toll money, the people of Dunwich repeatedly tried to close up the new channel and reopen the original one. The people of Walberswick fought back, and in 1342 raiders attacked the guardhouse that Dunwich had erected on Kings Holme, killing a toll collector.

Eventually, coastal erosion carried the day. The river mouth near Dunwich filled with silt, blocking the harbour and permanently diverting maritime traffic away from the town. As the population of Dunwich decreased, the town continued to fall into the sea. The last of its churches was abandoned in 1755 and fell in 1919.

COASTAL EROSION CONTINUES

Today the process of destruction continues unabated. The town is sited on sandy and chalky cliffs filled with slippery mica and rounded flint gravel. The high tides caused by storms continually weaken the lower sections of the cliff face. At the same time, a pattern of wind and sea-current action called longshore drift carries the coarse-grained sediment down the coastline from north to south. It is this combination of forces that have shifted the position of sandy Kings Holme.

Geologists estimate that the Dunwich coastline is receding by an average of 1 metre (3 feet) a year. In other words, the shore is now 2 km (1¼ miles) west of its location in Roman times. All that remains of proud and prosperous Dunwich is a small village with the ruins of Greyfriars Priory and of the 800-year-old chapel of the leper hospital. Geophysical surveys have detected buried masonry, probably from medieval structures, near the ruins of Greyfriars. They indicate that Greyfriars once formed part of a substantial establishment. However, the Suffolk Shoreline Management Plan estimates that the sea will claim the rest of Greyfriars within 70 years.

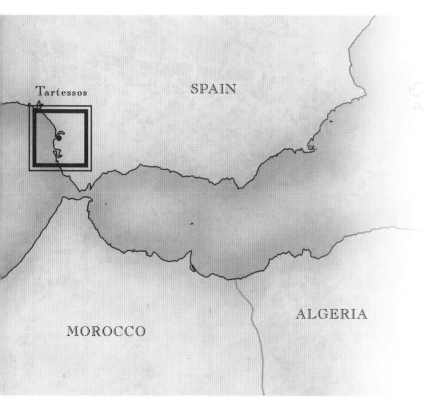

Tartessos – city of copper, silver and gold

Tartessos, a harbour city on the coast of what is now Andalusia in Spain, is a mystery. Though this ancient place is mentioned in the Bible, figured in an important Greek myth and is known to have been active in Bronze Age metal-trading, in the 6th century BCE the city disappeared. Though artefacts linked with the city have been found, the actual site is lost.

MYTHIC AND BIBLICAL TARTESSOS

In Greek myth, Tartessos is the site of one of the 12 labours of Hercules. The Greek hero's tenth labour required him to make a journey to the end of the world to bring back the red cattle belonging to the three-headed monster Geryon. At that time the 'end of the world' was considered to be to the west of Greece, beyond the Pillars of Hercules, now identified with the Straits of Gibraltar – in other words, the south-western coast of the Iberian Peninsula.

In the Old Testament, the city of Tarshish is mentioned as the place to which Jonah was fleeing when he was swallowed by the whale – a city that was noted for its large ships and its mineral wealth. Although the city of Tarsus in Turkey has also been suggested as the site of Tarshish, some biblical scholars point to Tartessos on the Spanish coast as the more likely identification.

BRONZE AGE TARTESSOS

Greek historical records say that Tartessos was located at the mouth of the Guadalquivir River. It was an important trading partner of the Phoenicians, who established the nearby city of Gades (modern-day Cadiz) in about 1100 BCE.

Tartessos' wealth came from its mineral resources, including gold, silver and copper from mines in Andalusia's Rio Tinto area, some of which date back to 3000 BCE. The anonymous Greek 'Pseudo-Scymnus', who wrote a geography of the ancient world in *c.* 90 BCE, described Tartessos as a 'famous town', whose riches came from the tin carried by the river from Celtica (the region in central Iberia settled by early Celtic peoples), as well as great quantities of gold and bronze. Copper and tin were especially valuable commodities during this period. They were the raw materials for the

manufacture of bronze, which was used to make tools, weapons, pots and pans, belt buckles and other necessities. Trading ships from Tartessos may also have discovered the route to the lucrative tin mines in Cornwall in the south-west of Britain.

According to the Greek historian Herodotus, the most important king of Tartessos was Arganthonios, who ruled from 640 to 550 BCE. His name means 'king of silver' in ancient Celtic. Another Greek historian, Strabo (*c.* 63 BCE–*c.* 24 CE) tells the story of a lost Greek sailor who was regally entertained by King Arganthonios and sent home laden with silver.

Below left *The Greeks believed Tartessos lay at the end of the world, on the south-western coast of the Iberian Peninsula beyond the Pillars of Hercules, now known as the Straits of Gibraltar.*

Right *Jonah was fleeing to Tarshish when he was swallowed by a whale, as is shown in this 17th-century engraving. Some scholars identify Tarshish with the lost city of Tartessos.*

WHAT HAPPENED TO TARTESSOS?

In the 6th century BCE, the city of Tartessos disappeared. Historians have proposed several explanations. In one theory, the city was destroyed by the Carthaginians, economically powerful traders centred in North Africa near the modern city of Tunis. According to this view, they attacked Tartessos in order to take over its lucrative trade routes.

Another theory states that other cultures, such as the Iberians, from whom Tartessos obtained metals for its trade with the Greeks and Phoenicians, began selling their metals directly to foreign markets. As its profitable trade faded,

Tartessos ceased to be an economic power and eventually disappeared.

In addition Tartessos may have been weakened by a natural disaster. Greek texts say that the city once lay between the two mouths of a river, though today there is only one river mouth. It may be that the delta of the Guadalquivir was gradually blocked off by a sandbar, burying ancient Tartessos under the shifting wetlands that have replaced the ancient estuaries behind the dunes at the river's mouth.

But perhaps the most intriguing theory for what happened to Tartessos

identifies the ancient city with Atlantis, the fabled civilization described by Plato. German physicist Rainer Kühne contends that satellite photos of southern Spain, taken in 2004, show rectangular structures and concentric circles that match well with Plato's description of the palaces and temples of Atlantis. In Plato's account the gods unleashed earthquakes and floods on the kingdom, sinking it into the sea in a single day. Kühne concurs, suggesting that Tartessos/Atlantis was destroyed by a flood that occurred between 800 and 500 BCE.

CHAPTER 2
CITIES OF THE DESERTS AND PLAINS

Some ancient cities of the deserts and plains were trade outposts and way stations. Frankincense caravans journeyed from Ubar to markets in Alexandria, Damascus and Jerusalem, and ideas travelled along with the goods. At their height, the oasis cities along China's Silk Road enjoyed a unique blending of Eastern and Western cultural elements.

Other cities functioned as administrative outposts. The monumental Roman buildings at Leptis Magna testify to the city's importance as a governmental centre of the Roman Empire in North Africa. The Aztec city of Tenochtitlan was the administrative and ritual hub of a network of tribute towns and agricultural districts in the valley of Mexico.

Floodplains of mighty rivers gave birth to many of the earliest civilizations. Ur, in Iraq, originated in the 6th millennium BCE. Even older is Çatalhöyük in southern Anatolia, a Neolithic settlement that dates back to around 7500 BCE. Some believe it is the oldest city in the world.

Oasis cities and mirage cities in the sky

The word 'oasis' conjures up the image of a shimmering patch of blue water in a desert landscape, complete with a welcoming nomad tent shaded by graceful date palms. Though the inviting image seems real enough, as travellers approach the vision recedes into the distance and weary voyagers can never reach it.

Among the world's lost cities, however, are many real oases: historical cities that provided water, food and recreation for trade caravans and other desert travellers. Loulan and Niya, oasis cities that once flourished along the Silk Road through China's forbidding Taklamakan Desert, have recently been discovered beneath the sands. Ubar, on the incense trade route across the Rub' al Khali Desert in the southern Arabian Peninsula, is another oasis city that has been found only recently, with the help of high-tech satellite images.

OASIS LEGENDS AND TRAVELLERS' TALES

Because of the magical beauty of oasis cities, legends and travellers' tales have grown up around many of them. According to one such legend, the Prophet Muhammad visited the oasis of al-Hasa in the eastern province of what is now Saudi Arabia. Hungry and tired, the Prophet asked a farmer if he could have a few dates and rest in the shade of the palms. As he served the dates, the farmer apologized for their withered appearance, explaining that the water supply at al-Hasa was almost exhausted. The Prophet ate the dates, rested a while and, as he was leaving, murmured a blessing: 'God bless the water of al-Hasa.' From that day, it is said, the oasis has always had a plentiful supply.

True to the Prophet Muhammad's prayer, al-Hasa today has 50–60 artesian springs that bring water to the surface from rock layers 150–185 metres (500–600 feet) below. Water is all it takes to make a desert bloom – water for people to drink; water to keep the date palms growing; water to channel into canals to irrigate crops and animal pastures. It is no wonder that oasis waters around the world have been reputed to possess miraculous powers. The waters of one of the smaller springs at al-Hasa, called Ain Najm, have a sulphurous quality long associated with healing. A legend dating back to the days when al-Hasa was under the rule of the Ottoman Turks states that Ain Najm was created by a falling star (in Arabic, *ain* means 'natural water source or spring', while *najm* means 'star'), which gave the spring its curative power.

Like al-Hasa, the oasis city of Farafra in the Libyan Desert of western Egypt has a walled date-palm grove and hot sulphur springs near by. Isolated in the desert, more than 200 km (125 miles) from its nearest neighbour, Farafra has been the focus of many legends. The Greek historian Herodotus tells the story of the mysterious disappearance of the army of Cambyses, the Persian king who conquered Egypt in the 6th century BCE. According to the story, 50,000 Persian soldiers were travelling from Thebes to the oasis of Siwa to destroy the oracle of Amun, which had predicted that Cambyses' African conquests would soon end. The soldiers were last seen in Farafra before striking off to cross the Great Sand Sea to the west. They never reached Siwa and were not seen again.

MIRAGES

The optical phenomenon that accounts for the vision of a desert oasis is a mirage. Like 'mirror', the word 'mirage' comes from the Latin *mirare*, which means 'to wonder at, admire'. Like a mirror image, a mirage occurs when light waves are bent to produce a representation of an object that is elsewhere. A mirage is not an optical illusion; it is a real phenomenon that can be photographed, like a rainbow. Mirage legends arise because the interpretation of the image is up to the fantasy-making powers of the human imagination.

Mirages can be divided into two categories. An 'inferior mirage' (so called because the image appears *beneath* the real object) is the most common. A thirsty traveller in the desert may see a bluish patch in the distance that looks like a pool of water. In reality, the image is a reflection of a real object – the blue sky. What happens is that the heat of the sand raises the temperature of the air near the ground so that it becomes

Above Greenland's geographical location and the clarity of the Arctic air create fascinating optical phenomena, such as this mirage pictured off the coast of Thule.

'A mirage is not an optical illusion; it is a real phenomenon that can be photographed, like a rainbow.'

less dense than the rest of the atmosphere. This variance bends light rays in an upward path, which the eye traces as the line of sight, so that the blue sky above appears on the ground. The same effect can often be seen on a sunny day on a hot roadway; as the sun warms the asphalt and the air above it, light is bent, making a pool of water shimmer on the road ahead.

MIRAGE CITIES IN THE SKY

The second, less-common type of mirage is called a 'superior mirage' (because the image appears *above* the true object). Visions of beautiful cities floating above the sea or above an Arctic ice field are the most impressive examples of this phenomenon. Superior mirages are also caused by a variance in air temperatures. When the

lower air is colder than the air above, as
often happens over water and large sheets of
ice, the light rays are bent downwards so that
images of distant objects appear to float in
the sky above. Superior mirages are more
stable than inferior mirages, often lasting for
several hours. Because of the curvature of
the Earth and the fact that light can travel
long distances very quickly, images from far
away – even from beyond the horizon – can
often be projected into the sky.

FAMOUS FLOATING CITIES

One of the most famous floating cities can
be seen in the Strait of Messina, between
Calabria on the toe of Italy's boot and the
island of Sicily. When conditions are right,
phantom castles, towers and fanciful spires –

as if from a fairytale – float miraculously in
the sky above the sea. The Italians call this
image the Fata Morgana, named after
Morgan le Fay, the shape-shifting fairy half-
sister of King Arthur. Similar visions have
been seen for centuries off the coast of
Ireland. Enchanted islands have been
reported as rising from the sea off the coasts
of Antrim, Donegal and Waterford.

Cities in the sky have also been seen in
Alaska and other regions of polar ice. In the
late 1880s an American prospector named
Willoughby photographed a mysterious
floating city that, according to Native
American legends, appeared each summer
near Mount Fairweather on the border
between Alaska and Canada's Yukon
Territory. The photograph clearly shows the

city's house fronts and church steeples. Willoughby's vision was confirmed by other observers. In 1889 the *New York Times* quoted L.B. French as having seen houses, streets and large buildings, either mosques or cathedrals, near Mount Fairweather. That same year *The Times* reported that the city in Willoughby's photograph had been identified as Bristol in England, more than 4,000 km (2,500 miles) away!

Famed explorer Robert E. Peary, the first man to reach the North Pole, had his own encounter with a phantom floating city. In June 1906 Peary was studying the horizon from the summit of Cape Colgate in north-western North America when he saw an unknown land lying 195 km (120 miles) offshore. He named the mysterious place 'Crocker Land' after one of the financial backers of his expedition. Peary's report was so convincing that the New York Museum of Natural History sent an expedition to explore Crocker Land. Native Americans travelling with the explorers were dubious, calling the vision a *poojok*, which means 'mist'. Though they saw the same vision, the explorers realized that they (like Peary) had indeed been fooled by a mirage.

There are many reports of sailors seeing floating cities. One of the best-documented examples took place in July 1943 in the Mediterranean Sea east of Malta, when 93 US Navy sailors – the entire crew of a ship – saw a city floating in the sky. Sailors described the fantastic beauty of the city's white marble buildings, gardens and tree-filled parks. Many people, including children and dogs, could be seen walking, playing and sitting on lawns. The mirage, which seemed to keep pace with the ship, lasted for several hours.

A similar mirage was reported in China. On Sunday 7 May 2006, when the town was thronged with vacationers, the vision of a city with modern high-rise buildings, broad streets, cars and crowds of pedestrians appeared off the coast of Penglai, on the tip of the Shandong Peninsula. The mirage, which was witnessed by thousands of tourists and local residents, lasted more than four hours and was photographed for the China News Service. Experts say that two days of soaking rain help to explain the phenomenon, but other sources say that many mirages have previously been seen in Penglai, which has been known for centuries as a dwelling place of the gods.

Left *A grove of date palms provides some refreshing shade at the Farafra Oasis in the Libyan Desert of western Egypt. Today, about 5,000 Bedouins live in the village near by.*

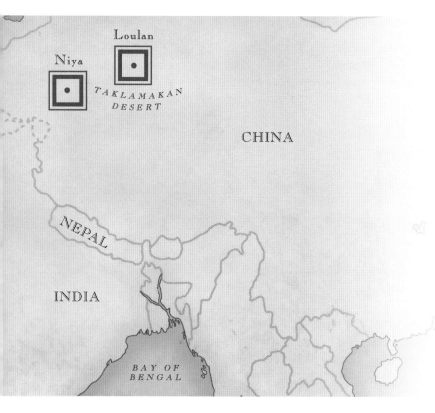

Loulan and Niya – desert oases on the Silk Road

The Silk Road was a series of trade routes that linked China with the civilizations of the West. Stretching for more than 5,000 miles (8,000 km) and in active use for more than 2,000 years, the routes spread cultural, artistic and religious ideas as well as goods.

Along the road are the ruins of Loulan, Niya and other ancient cities that once served as oases and market towns, and which have only recently been discovered beneath the desert sands.

LOULAN

Loulan was founded on the north-eastern edge of the Taklamakan Desert in the 2nd century BCE. The discovery in 1980 of a female mummy, thought to be 3,800 years old, suggests that the site may have been inhabited for many more years.

At its height, Loulan was the eastern gateway to the Taklamakan Desert crossing. In 139 BCE the Chinese emperor Wu Ti sent an envoy out on the Silk Road to seek an alliance with the people of what is now Uzbekistan. Sixteen years later the envoy returned with news of the riches of the west, the new faith of Buddhism and a breed of horses that would benefit the emperor's army. Passing through Loulan, the envoy recorded that the city had 1,570 households and 14,100 residents. The surrounding land was sandy and salty and the people lived primarily by herding donkeys, horses and

camels. Over the next years ten caravans a year travelled through Loulan from the emperor's court to the cities of central Asia.

In the 4th century the Tarim River, which supplied water to the Loulan region, changed course. As water became scarce,

Loulan was abandoned and by the 6th century it had disappeared into the shifting desert sands. It lay hidden until two 19th-century adventurers – Sven Hedin, a Swedish explorer and geographer, and Aurel Stein, a Hungarian-British adventurer – mounted

ARCHEOLOGY FROM SPACE

Though overland archeological expeditions have continued to explore the buried cities of the Taklamakan, interest in the region has soared due to exciting new technology. Operated from the NASA Space Shuttle, Shuttle Imaging Radar (SIR) produces radar-frequency images of the Earth's surface. The images are especially effective in locating desert ruins because they can identify objects buried in 3 metres (10 feet) of dry, fine sand.

An SIR image taken by the Space Shuttle *Endeavour* during its 106th orbit on 16 April 1994 shows the ruins of Niya. Scientists believe that a diagonal line from the upper left to the lower right of the image is a canal, which may have channelled irrigation water from the now-dry River Niya. Mottled white and purple areas are the river's low-lying floodplains. Dark green and black areas are dunes that once confined the river's flow.

separate expeditions to the region. Both men suffered incredible hardships. In his 1898 book *Through Asia*, Hedin describes his disastrous 1896 expedition on which most of the party, including all the pack camels, died of thirst and heat exposure. Hedin and two companions managed to crawl to a Taklamakan oasis and were rescued by a passing caravan.

Hedin's discovery of Loulan in 1899 inspired Aurel Stein to organize four expeditions to the region between 1900 and 1930. At Loulan, Stein found fragments of silk and damask that shed light on 2,000-year-old Chinese manufacturing techniques and tapestries with pictures of Greek gods, underscoring the mingling of Western and Eastern cultures along the Silk Road.

NIYA

From Loulan, the oldest part of the Silk Road continues west, along the southern edge of the Taklamakan Desert. Niya, the westernmost town of the ancient Shanshan kingdom, lies 600 km (370 miles) west of Loulan. Like that city, Niya was once a cosmopolitan market town, where ideas, languages and religions were exchanged along with trade goods. On an expedition to Niya, Aurel Stein discovered tatters of antique rugs, pottery jars decorated with people, animals and mythological beings, and even some furniture, including an elaborately carved armchair with lion's claw legs, that displayed Greek influences.

Niya suffered a similar fate to Loulan. The end for the oasis city arrived when the spring-fed rivers that supplied water to the region dried up or shifted course. As the water disappeared, so did the town, which was abandoned and eventually reclaimed by the expanding Taklamakan Desert.

Below *The remains of Niya lie on the southern edge of the Tarim Basin in modern Xinjiang, China. An important oasis city on the south branch of the Silk Road, Niya has been reclaimed by the desert.*

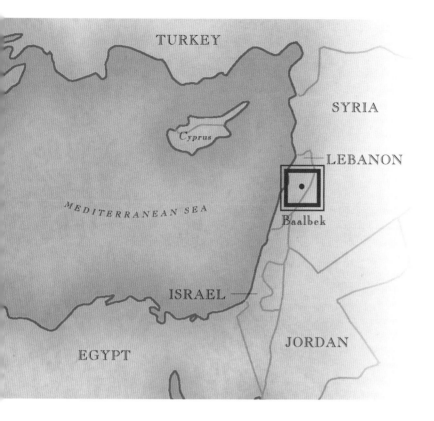

Baalbek – Roman city of the sun

The temple complex of Baalbek stands at a high point in the fertile Bekaa Valley, about 88 km (55 miles) north-east of Beirut in Lebanon. During Roman times the town was known as Heliopolis – 'city of the sun' – and was the site of the largest religious structure ever built by Rome: the massive Temple of Jupiter Heliopolitan.

Though mainstream archeology holds that this enormous temple and its platform base were built by the legions of Julius Caesar, who settled in Baalbek in 15 BCE, the gigantic foundation stones beneath the temple hint that the site has a more mysterious history.

HISTORY AND CONSTRUCTION

The conventional view is that Baalbek dates back some 5,000 years. Excavations beneath the Great Court of the Temple of Jupiter have uncovered traces of civilizations from as far back as the early Bronze Age (2900–2300 BCE). Later, the Phoenicians chose Baalbek as the site for a temple to their sun god Baal. After the death of Alexander the Great in 323 BCE, the city was ruled successively by the Seleucid kings of Syria and the Ptolemaic kings of Egypt. In 15 BCE Heliopolis, as the city was called by the Greeks and Egyptians, came under Roman rule.

Over the next three centuries, under a succession of Roman emperors, Baalbek's major temples to Jupiter, Bacchus and Venus were constructed. The immense Jupiter temple, which was completed in 60 CE, is

lined with 104 granite columns imported from Aswan in Egypt. The Temple of Bacchus, Greek god of wine and fertility, built during the 2nd century, is today the best-preserved Roman temple in the world. The circular Venus temple, adorned with seashells, doves and other symbols of the ancient love goddess, was built during the 3rd century.

One of the great mysteries of archeology concerns the foundation stones beneath the Temple of Jupiter, which stands on a platform called the Grand Terrace. The outer wall of the foundation of this terrace is constructed of massive, finely crafted and perfectly positioned blocks of stone. Each weighs about 408 tonnes (400 tons). Above these is another layer of visible stones, three of which – called the Trilithon – weigh more than 907 tonnes (890 tons) each. Another, even larger, dressed stone lies in a quarry 0.4 km (¼ mile) away, presumably waiting to be transported to the site. This stone, called the Stone of the Pregnant Woman, weighs about 1,088 tonnes (1,070 tons), making it the largest piece of stonework in the world.

What makes these massive stones so mysterious is that there are no known technologies in the ancient world – or even today – that would be capable of the transportation and precise placement of these stones, given the amount of working space and the terrain between the quarry and the site. Moreover, though the Baalbek temple complex has been written about since ancient times, no accounts link the placement of these stones to the Romans. Though it runs counter to accepted archeological chronology, some speculate that the placement of these stones may date back to a technologically advanced lost civilization from the Palaeolithic period. This theory is cited to explain why the Phoenicians, and later the Romans, chose Baalbek for their temples.

COLLAPSE AND EXCAVATION

The temples of Baalbek served as a place of worship and pilgrimage until the end of the 4th century. With the coming of Christianity, the city declined in importance. Conquest by the Islamic and Ottoman Empires and an earthquake in the mid-1700s further

degraded the site. Today the town of Baalbek, which is connected by road to Beirut and to Damascus in Syria, has about 30,000 residents.

The ruins at Baalbek have been visited for centuries. Arab historians and geographers described the Roman buildings as early as the 9th century. European travellers have been visiting the remains since the 16th century. The first scientific work on the site was done in 1757 by English researchers James Dawkins and Robert Wood and in 1785 by French researcher Louis François Cassas. In the 19th century, Baalbek was a frequent destination for travelling artists, poets and photographers.

Since those days, researchers have been drawn to Baalbek by the monumental scale of its structures and their marvellous blend of Near Eastern and Greco-Roman art and architecture. After a visit in 1898 by German emperor Wilhelm II, major work on the site was undertaken by German archeologists.

Since 1945 Lebanon has directed its own antiquities research at the site. Excavation around the stairway of the Temple of Jupiter has uncovered the remains of a colonnaded street. A previously unknown temple, known as the Temple of the Muses, has also been discovered near the Temple of Venus. Further work may unearth other treasures and clues to Baalbek's mysterious past.

Above Remains of altars and ritual pools can still be seen in the Great Court at Baalbek, testifying to the importance of the site. A tower once stood at the centre of the courtyard, flanked by two granite columns.

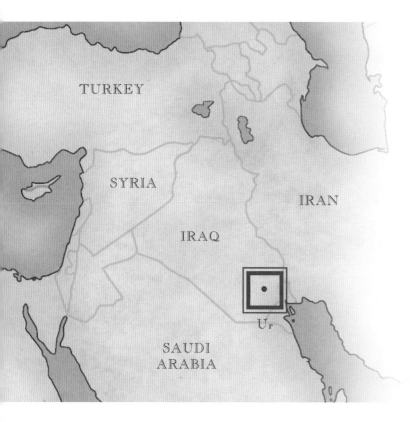

TURKEY

SYRIA

IRAN

IRAQ

SAUDI
ARABIA

Ur

Ur – metropolis of the cradle of civilization

Located near the original mouth of the Euphrates River on the Persian Gulf, Ur was a thriving metropolitan centre in southern Mesopotamia, dating back to the 6th millennium BCE. Some archeologists believe that at its height, from c. 2030 to 1980 BCE, Ur was the largest city in the world, with a population of between 30,000 and 65,000 people.

Although Ur prospered in times of peace and war until around 500 BCE, today its location near the city of Nasiriyah in Iraq, south of Baghdad, has brought new wars to its doorstep, threatening the existence of its spectacular ruins.

UR AND ITS TREASURES
Some biblical scholars identify Ur as the city mentioned in the book of Genesis as the birthplace of Abraham, considered to be a patriarch of Judaism, Christianity and Islam. In Genesis, God tells Abraham to leave his home in Ur to travel to the Promised Land, where he will be the 'father of many'.

In the first half of the 3rd millennium BCE, Ur developed from a simple agricultural settlement into a powerful city. Because the area was relatively poor in resources, the town's favourable position near land and sea routes spurred a lively international trade that linked Ur to the commercial, artistic and cultural centres of the ancient world. Ur's growth was also aided by climate change during this period. Archeologists believe that because of increasing drought, small villages had to consolidate into larger urban

centres that could provide the large-scale irrigation networks essential for agriculture.

As the city grew, Ur's kings became the rulers of the entire kingdom of Sumeria. Many elaborate tombs filled with treasures were constructed for its kings and queens, as well as temples to the city's principal deity, the Sumerian moon god Nanna. Ur continued to prosper under a succession of ruling dynasties. Sargon of Akkad conquered the city around 2340 BCE. Ur-Nammu, who ruled the city between *c.* 2112 and 2094 BCE, built many spectacular monuments and temples, including the Great Ziggurat – a temple tower sacred to Nanna. Still largely intact, the tower stands on a rectangular base, with its four corners oriented to the points of the compass. The terraced pyramid on top, rising 15 metres (50 feet) above the desert plain, was constructed of sun-baked brick reinforced by reed matting.

By the end of the 3rd millennium the brilliance and material affluence of Ur began to wane. After falling in succession to the Akkadians, the Elamites, the Babylonians and the Persian Empire, Ur declined in importance. Climate changes, which had

stimulated its early growth, also contributed to its collapse. Increasing drought, a shift in the course of the River Euphrates and the silting of the outlet to the Persian Gulf cut off the flow of life-giving water. By 500 BCE the city was abandoned. Today, its ruins lie 16 km (10 miles) away from the Euphrates river bed.

DISCOVERY AND EXCAVATION
Though Ur was visited by Western explorers as early as the 17th century, the first excavation was made by British Consul J.E. Taylor in the 1850s. Taylor uncovered parts of the Ziggurat and found clay-baked cylinders that identified the city as Ur. Between 1922 and 1934, British archeologist Sir Charles Woolley, leading a team from London's British Museum and the University of Pennsylvania, excavated more than 1,600 burial sites at Ur, including 16 'royal tombs' dating to about 2600 BCE. The tombs contained incredible treasures, including gold and silver vessels decorated with lapis lazuli, carnelian, agate, chalcedony and other gems, tools and weapons, jewellery and personal belongings. They also included

'The tombs contained incredible treasures, including gold and silver vessels decorated with gems, tools and weapons, jewellery and personal belongings.'

cylinder seals and other evidence in cuneiform (Sumerian) writing that conveyed a wealth of information about Ur at its height. Many of these treasures are today housed in the British Museum and the University of Pennsylvania Museum of Archaeology and Anthropology.

UR TODAY

Under Saddam Hussein, the Talil Air Base was established adjacent to the site of Ur's ruins. Iraqi soldiers from the base fled through the ruins from the advance of US forces during the 2003 invasion. In addition to the Great Ziggurat and the now-cleared royal tombs, the whole site remains rich in deposits of broken pottery and other archeological debris. The ruins are now under the protection of Coalition forces and the US military, but Western archeologists continue to be concerned about the security of the site.

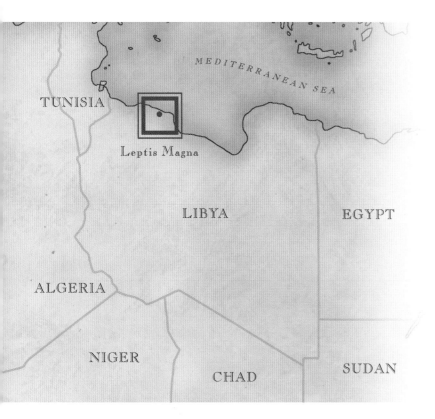

Leptis Magna – Rome in North Africa

Leptis Magna is an ancient city on the Mediterranean coast of North Africa, near the modern-day city of Al Khums in Libya. For more than 600 years it was an important administrative base for the Roman Empire.

Covered by sand since it was abandoned in the 6th century, the site contains some of the best-preserved 2nd- and 3rd-century Roman buildings in the world. Buried treasures continue to emerge from the sands, including a spectacular Roman mosaic unearthed in September 2000.

PAST GLORY

Leptis Magna was founded by Phoenician colonists in the 10th century BCE. Phoenician sailors used its natural harbour protected by islands as a regular point of call on their trade route across the region. From the 6th century BCE the city was ruled by Carthage, then a major power in the Mediterranean. After Rome defeated Carthage in the Second Punic War in 202 BCE, Leptis became a colony of the Roman Empire with full Roman citizenship rights for its population.

In the 2nd and 3rd centuries, Leptis achieved special prominence when Lucius Septimius Severus, who was born in the city, became Emperor of Rome. He favoured his home town by commissioning many important buildings, and he even visited the city in 205. Among the emperor's building projects were a magnificent new forum (public meeting space), a four-way arch at the city's main intersection and colonnades to line the broad avenue leading to the harbour. An underground system was constructed to carry water to elegant private villas and Roman baths.

Under Roman rule, Leptis had virtual autonomy. The city prospered, since Rome protected the surrounding countryside from bandit raids and kept peace among local tribal groups. As the Mediterranean port of the Roman trade route through the Sahara and into the African interior, Leptis became a lively international market town as well as a profitable exporter of local products, especially grain and olives. The opening of a limestone quarry south of the city provided stone to build later structures, including an aqueduct, a luxurious bathhouse and a large circus (racetrack).

Right One of the Roman-era mosaics recently unearthed at Leptis Magna depicts a weary gladiator staring at his slain opponent. The mosaics have been praised for their exceptional clarity and feeling.

DECLINE AND FALL

As the power of the Roman Empire waned and trade declined, Leptis, too, began to fade. By the 4th century, North African desert tribes were regularly raiding the countryside around the city, though Leptis itself was protected by its Roman walls.

Then, in 439, a Germanic tribe called the Vandals captured Carthage from the Romans and took control of Leptis. The Vandal leader Gaiseric ordered the city's walls to be demolished to prevent the citizens from rebelling against Vandal rule. With no walls to protect it, the city was sacked by the Berbers in 523. Though Leptis enjoyed a brief resurgence as a provincial capital of the Byzantine Empire, it never recovered its former glory. By the time of the Arab conquest of North Africa in the 650s, the city was virtually abandoned.

DISCOVERIES

In the 1920s and 1930s, when Libya was an Italian colony, Italian archeologists began to excavate Leptis Magna. After the Second World War British archeologists started working at the site and discovered many Roman remains. Particularly well preserved are the elegant public baths that were built by the Emperor Hadrian, as well as the forum and basilica (assembly hall) built by Emperor Septimius Severus.

But perhaps the most wonderful find was unearthed in the ruins of a villa that once housed Roman gladiators. On the floor of the athletes' cold-water bathhouse, 3.6 metres (12 feet) deep in the sandy soil, archeologists from the University of Hamburg discovered a spectacular 2,000-year-old mosaic that has been called the finest example of the art form to have survived. In tiny chips of green, brown and gold glass and stone, the mosaic's scenes depict four young men wrestling a wild bull, a warrior in combat with a deer, a fatigued gladiator resting near the opponent he has killed and a startling realistic portrait of a slain gladiator, with his head tilting backwards, which has been hailed as a masterpiece. Although the mosaic was first uncovered in 2000, news of the discovery was not released until 2005, to keep it safe until it could be moved to a small museum near by.

Less than one-third of the 607 hectares (1,500 acres) of the Leptis Magna site has been excavated. Many other exciting artistic and historical finds may still await discovery.

Left This view of the basilica, one the major projects of Septimius Severus, shows its two colossal columns, standing on pedestals. Building began in 209 CE and was completed in 216 by Septimius' son, Caracalla.

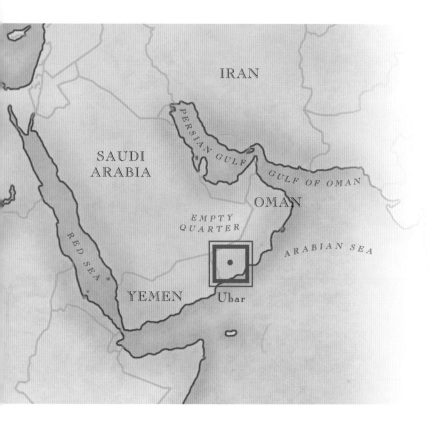

Ubar – Atlantis of the sands

Ubar, sometimes called Iram of the Pillars, was an oasis and trading outpost on the incense trade route across the Rub' al Khali Desert in the southern Arabian Peninsula. Dubbed 'the Atlantis of the Sands' by T.E. Lawrence (Lawrence of Arabia), Ubar was known for centuries only from legends, folk tales and mentions in the Qur'an and the Arabian Nights.

Though many explorers have searched for the city, its ruins were conclusively identified only recently at Shis'r in present-day Oman with the assistance of high-tech satellite images and space shuttle-based remote-sensing technology.

THE LEGEND

Legend says that Ubar was a vast city of gold that disappeared in an instant about 2,000 years ago. Bedouin folk tales confirm the city's mysterious disappearance, but describe Ubar as a trading centre famed for its frankincense, a sweet-smelling incense used in perfumes, medicines and ritual embalming of the dead. In the ancient world, frankincense was as rare and valuable as gold. Made from resin tapped from Boswellia trees in the nearby Qara Mountains, the frankincense was taken by camel caravan from Ubar to markets in Alexandria, Jerusalem, Damascus and the western end of the Mediterranean. Trade in frankincense helped Ubar grow from a small oasis town to a prosperous walled city.

The Qur'an says that Ubar was founded by the tribe of Ad, the great-grandchildren of Noah. Though it was a fabulous 'many-columned city' unlike any other in Arabia, its inhabitants were rich and sinful people, who were rumoured to practise black magic. When Ubar's King Shaddad defied the warnings of the prophet Hud, Allah destroyed the city with a 'divine shout' and Ubar sank without a trace into the desert sands, some time between 300 and 500 CE.

Archeological excavation has confirmed some of these stories. Ruins show that the town was a kind of fortress, with walls and towers to protect its water supply and valuable trade goods from raiding nomadic tribes. The find of small crystals of frankincense confirms Ubar's importance in incense trading. Analysis of bones and vegetable remains indicates that its people raised sheep, goats and other domestic animals and used grinding stones to prepare barley, dates and other local produce grown with the help of irrigation.

SEARCH AND DISCOVERY

Many renowned explorers have searched for Ubar in the mysterious 'Empty Quarter' of the Arabian Peninsula – a vast, open area with sand dunes more than 183 metres (600 feet) high. T.E. Lawrence wrote about Ubar, but died before he could lead his own expedition to find it. In the 1930s and 1940s Bertram Thomas, British envoy to the Sultan of Oman and the first European to cross the Rub' al Khali Desert, and Sir Wilfred Thesiger, British explorer and travel writer, searched unsuccessfully for Ubar. The first hint of discovery came in 1953, when a team led by British explorer Sir Ranulph Fiennes, following camel trails through the quarter, came upon the ruins of a fort previously identified as dating from the 16th century at a place called Shis'r.

HIGH-TECH AND LOW-TECH EXPLORATION

In the 1980s Los Angeles film-maker and amateur archeologist Nicholas Clapp began researching and planning his own expedition in the hope of finding and filming the lost city. Clapp's team made use of the latest high-tech tools, including satellite images and Shuttle Imaging Radar (SIR). The images showed distinct tracks through the desert, which marked the old

Left *The ruins of an ancient city on the frankincense trade route in southern Oman have been identified with the fabled city of Ubar. At its height, the city was an oasis with date gardens and a fort.*

'When Ubar's King Shaddad defied the warnings of the prophet Hud, Allah destroyed the city with a 'divine shout' and Ubar sank without a trace into the desert sands.'

caravan routes. The routes were found to converge at Shis'r.

The identification of the site was further confirmed through the study of ancient maps, descriptions and written accounts by earlier explorers, including Thomas and Thesiger. Clapp and his team, which included Sir Ranulph Fiennes and German-American archeologist Dr Juris Zarins, excavated the area around Shis'r in 1990 and 1991. They uncovered a large octagonal fortress with thick walls 3 metres (10 feet) high and eight tall towers at the corners. Greek, Roman and Syrian pottery, some dating back 4,000 years, indicated that the site was indeed a major trade centre and probably the legendary Ubar.

The excavation also seems to have solved the mystery of the city's destruction. A giant limestone cavern to store water was discovered beneath the fortress. As the people of Ubar used the water and the water level in the cavern dropped, the cavern walls may have collapsed, causing large portions of the city to sink into the desert, just as the legends said.

The story of the rediscovery of Ubar illustrates the working methodology that is employed by many of the contemporary archeologists. The new approach combines the use of high-tech tools, such as remote-sensing imagery, with the study of geology, climate and plant and animal life, as well as ancient manuscripts. This interdisciplinary methodology allows researchers to gain real insight into the lives of ancient peoples and thus to better understand the sites they are studying.

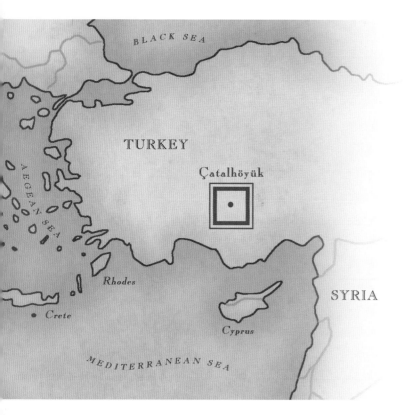

Çatalhöyük – oldest city in the world

Çatalhöyük was a very large Neolithic settlement, which some archeologists believe may be the world's oldest city. The site in southern Anatolia in Turkey, near present-day Konya, dates back to around 7500 BCE. Discovered in 1958, Çatalhöyük is today the subject of exploration by a team of more than 100 archeologists, scientists and specialists from all over the world.

Excavation work has already yielded some surprising new discoveries that challenge previous assumptions about the culture of Çatalhöyük.

LIFE IN ÇATALHÖYÜK

Houses for the 3,000–8,000 people who lived in Çatalhöyük were tightly packed together in a honeycomb-like maze, so that there were few or no streets. Areas between houses served as middens – dumps for garbage, including sewage, food waste and wood ash from cooking fires. Access to the houses was across the roofs, which were constructed of wood and reeds plastered with mud, and down stairs.

Individual households of five to ten people seem to have been the primary social unit of the culture, as there is no evidence of public spaces, administrative buildings or elite households, such as dwellings for kings or priests. Each house had its own hearth, oven, storage rooms and workrooms. Each family also seems to have buried its dead under special platforms in the house's main room. The interior walls of the houses were rich with artwork, mural paintings and sculptures. Wall paintings depict hunting scenes and wild animals, including images of the now extinct auroch (a type of cattle), stags and vultures swooping down on headless human figures. Evidence shows that heads of animals were mounted on the walls.

Although no remains of temples have been found, artefacts suggest that the religion of Çatalhöyük was rich in symbols. Distinctive baked clay figurines, long thought to represent the Mother Goddess, occupied wall niches and were placed in grain-storage bins, probably as a means of ritual protection.

The settlement's location, on the east bank of the River Carsamba, provided water and wet marshes – a source of wild food, including fish, wildfowl eggs and mammals (attracted by the water) that could be hunted. The marshes also provided reeds, mud and other construction materials. Archeological evidence suggests that the town engaged in long-distance trade of items such as storage baskets from Mesopotamia, shells from the Red Sea and Mediterranean, and obsidian for tools from Cappadocia to the north-east. Most necessities of life,

THE MOTHER GODDESS ENIGMA

Some researchers now think that the 'Mother Goddess' figurines found by Mellaart and others at the site may also represent bears. They believe that religious practice in Çatalhöyük was centred around household shrines filled with images from nature, including paintings and sculptures of leopards, bears and other wild animals. However, the bear is also an ancient symbol of the Mother Goddess, connected with the mysteries of birth and death. The find of a plastered bull skull and bull horns as ritual items – also symbols of the Goddess – suggests that the mystery of Çatalhöyük will continue to unfold.

however, were produced locally, including food crops such as wheat, peas and lentils and domesticated sheep and goats.

One of the most distinctive features of the Çatalhöyük site is its layering. When a house reached the end of its useful life, people demolished the roof and walls and carefully filled in the lower half of the house to create the foundation for a new dwelling on the same spot. Archeologists have found at least 14 levels of habitation in the largest mound on the site (in Turkish, *çatal* means 'fork' and *höyük* means 'mound'), built one on top of the other.

DISCOVERY AND RECENT FINDS

Çatalhöyük was first identified and excavated in the late 1950s and early 1960s by British archeologist James Mellaart. He excavated about 160 buildings and brought the attention of the world to the site's extraordinary wall paintings and clay figurines. Among his most important finds were a wall painting that shows a town (possibly Çatalhöyük) in the foreground and the eruption of a twin-peaked volcano (perhaps the nearby Hasan Dag) in the background. Mellaart also found many clay figurines, which he assumed represented the Mother Goddess, including a seated figure flanked by two lions, which had been placed in a grain bin, perhaps to ensure the harvest or to protect the food supply.

Since 1993 work at Çatalhöyük has been carried out by an international team under the direction of Ian Hodder, professor of anthropology at Stanford University. Among the new discoveries is a beautifully made stamp seal that shows an animal, probably a bear, with its front and hind legs raised upwards. The stamp was in all likelihood used to create designs on skin or clothing.

Above A shelter protects excavations in the south area of Çatalhöyük. The wealth of archeological evidence found here makes the settlement the largest and most sophisticated Neolithic site yet uncovered.

'The religion of Çatalhöyük was rich in symbols, such as the baked clay figurines that have long been thought to represent the Mother Goddess.'

Mohenjo-Daro – a planned city in the Indus Valley

Mohenjo-Daro is the most important city of the Indus civilization that flourished on the plain between the Indus and Ghaggar-Hakra Rivers between 2600 and 1900 BCE. Its ruins were discovered in the 1920s in what today is Sindh province, Pakistan.

Right *Mohenjo-Daro is by far the largest of the discovered cities of the Indus civilization. Its planned layout is based on a grid of streets, with structures built of baked mud, sun-dried bricks and burned timbers.*

Streets and buildings were laid out along the lines of a regular grid, making Mohenjo-Daro perhaps the earliest example of urban planning.

A PLANNED METROPOLIS

Mohenjo-Daro was the largest city of the Indus Valley, with as many as 35,000 residents. It was situated on a ridge that sits like an island above the floodplain of the Indus River. From this strategic location it probably dominated the network of river trade moving inland from the coast of the Arabian Sea. The variety of raw materials found at the site, including copper, shell and ivory, indicates that the city was linked by trade to distant resource areas.

The buildings at Mohenjo-Daro were made of kiln-fired brick. Most of the houses had a central courtyard surrounded by several rooms and stairs leading to an upper storey; they also had their own well. Originally the city was shaped like a square, with 12 main streets of beaten earth dividing the town into a dozen blocks. Eleven of the blocks were residential, containing closely packed houses, shops and workshops; the 12th block, now known as the Citadel, was the administrative and public centre of the city. Its ruins include the Great Bath, a large colonnaded building with a water tank; the Granary, a massive public building that could have been a storehouse, a temple or an administrative building; and the Assembly Hall. Today the Citadel is topped by the *stupa* (tower shrine) of a Buddhist monastery dating to the 2nd century.

ECONOMY AND GOVERNMENT

The fertile floodplain surrounding the city provided an environment suitable for growing cereal crops, grazing domesticated animals and for fishing, hunting and the gathering of wild plants. Platforms for pounding grain, storage space for wheat and rice, and air ducts that may have been used to dry the grain also suggest a high level of economic organization. Craft workshops engaged in copper work, shell and ivory carving and stone-tool production, as well as the manufacture of pottery and ornaments.

Left The expression of the 'Priest-King', a sculpture found at Mohenjo-Daro, seems to indicate governmental or religious authority. The decorated robe suggests ritual clothing.

Among Mohenjo-Daro's unique artworks were finely carved stone seals decorated with animal motifs and writing, which may have been used as counters in trade transactions.

Small stone carvings of seated male figures may offer clues about the city's government. One statue in particular, known today as the 'Priest-King', has a neatly trimmed beard, a narrow headband, an armband and a cloak decorated with a trefoil pattern embellished with red pigment. Though there is no evidence that Mohenjo-Daro was ruled by a king or priest, the statue's self-possessed and somewhat haughty expression suggests that he may be wearing ceremonial attire.

Mohenjo-Daro's favourable position near the Indus River may have contributed to its decline. Today the Indus has shifted position and flows to the east of the city site, while the Ghaggar-Hakra River is dry. These changes suggest that flooding may have interfered with agriculture and contributed to the city's decline. By 1900 BCE the great metropolis of Mohenjo-Daro was all but abandoned.

DISCOVERY AND EXCAVATION

Mohenjo-Daro was discovered in 1922 by R.D. Banerji, an officer belonging to the Archaeological Survey of India. During the 1930s there were excavations at the site, undertaken by a number of British and Indian researchers. Between 1944 and 1948 Sir Mortimer Wheeler, who at that time was Director General of Archaeology in India, conducted extensive excavations at Mohenjo-Daro. Together, these early researchers produced a remarkable amount of information that is still being studied by scholars today.

The last major dig at Mohenjo-Daro took place in the mid-1960s, after which the focus of work at the site shifted to conserving the exposed structures from weathering. The earliest habitation levels of the site now lie below the underground water table, and many of the city's mysteries may remain buried in the sand. More answers about this important site and the Indus civilization may still materialize when the writing on the beautiful stone seals is finally deciphered.

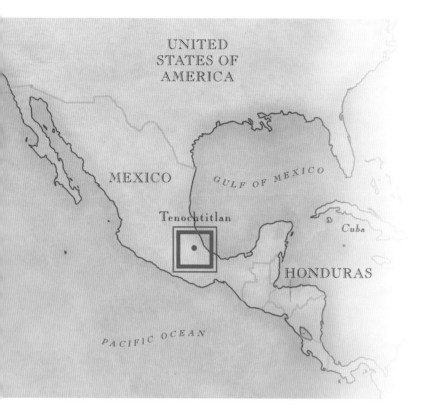

UNITED STATES OF AMERICA

MEXICO

GULF OF MEXICO

Tenochtitlan

Cuba

HONDURAS

PACIFIC OCEAN

Tenochtitlan – fall and rediscovery

The fall of the great Aztec capital of Tenochtitlan to the Spanish conquistadors in 1521 was recorded in written accounts by Hernán Cortés and members of his army, and was also illustrated in a pictorial document created by Native American artists in c. 1560. These remarkable documents chronicle an epic event in Meso-American history.

The rediscovery of the ruins of the 14th-century city of Tenochtitlan beneath the streets of modern-day Mexico City is no less remarkable. As has happened in many past civilizations, a new city was simply layered over an ancient one.

CORTÉS AND MOTECUHZOMA

After exploring the coast of the Yucatan Peninsula, Cortés and his tiny Spanish Army established a garrison at Veracruz. The Aztec king, Motecuhzoma, who had been monitoring the movements of these strange visitors, had sent emissaries and lavish gifts, but these offerings only convinced Cortés that there were fabulous riches to be had by conquering Tenochtitlan.

As they marched towards Tenochtitlan, the Spanish Army won several battles against Native American warriors. Many defeated warriors were persuaded to join the Spanish cause, against a city to which they had long been forced to pay tribute in men, goods and sacrificial victims. When the Spanish and their allies reached the southern causeway to the island city, Motecuhzoma himself came out to meet them. In an attempt to appease the Spanish, or perhaps to trap them within the city where they would be outnumbered, Motecuhzoma invited the visitors into Tenochtitlan and housed them in an old palace in the middle of the capital.

After two weeks spent as Motecuhzoma's honoured guests, the Spanish asked for an audience with the king and then took him hostage in the midst of his own city! Although the king continued to conduct affairs of state from a guarded apartment, the end was near. Aztec warriors, who saw certain defeat in Motecuhzoma's policy of appeasement, attacked the Spanish with stones and darts. The Spanish fought back with cannons. Motecuhzoma himself was mortally wounded by his own warriors as he tried to stop the fighting. Seizing the advantage, the Spanish charged up the steps of the Templo Mayor and cast down the images of the Aztec gods – an ultimate sign of victory, in Aztec belief.

Since their position within the city was indefensible, Cortés and his men attempted a daring night escape. The Spanish soldiers were strung out along the causeway when they were attacked by Aztec warriors in canoes. Though many died in what is called *La Noche Triste* (the sad night), the Spanish managed to regroup on the plain and lay siege to the city. A naval blockade isolated Tenochtitlan, at the same time as a raging smallpox epidemic (the contagion having been brought into the city by the Spanish) weakened the Aztec population. After 93 days the Aztec leader Cuauhtemoc surrendered to Cortés, bringing an end to Tenochtitlan and the Aztec Empire.

REDISCOVERY BENEATH THE CITY STREETS

Most of Tenochtitlan remained buried under the growing Spanish capital until 1790, when excavation for water pipes uncovered the Sun Stone and the statue of Coaticue, the Aztec Mother Goddess. The statue was reburied by the Dominican priests, who feared its effect on the Native American residents.

Then, on 1 February 1978, some electrical workers excavating a trench at 1.8 metres (6 feet) below street level, to the north-west of the cathedral, encountered a large carved

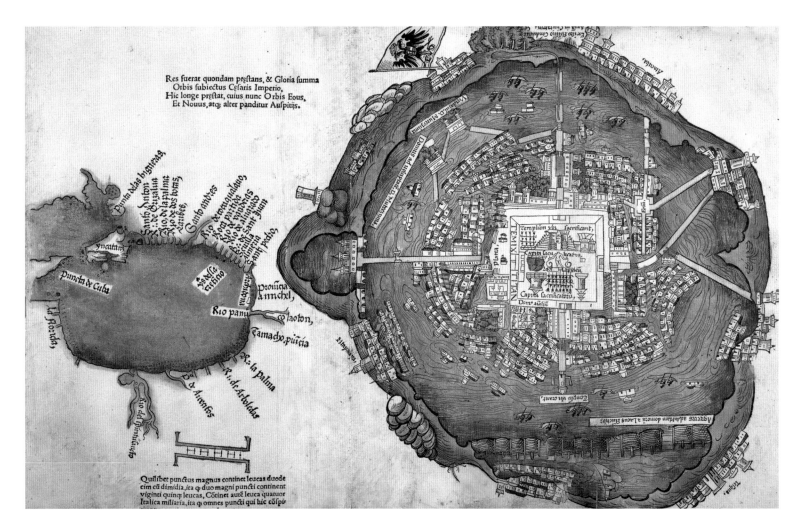

Res fuerat quondam præstans, & Gloria summa
Orbis subiectus Cæsaris Imperio,
Hic longe præstat, cuius nunc Orbis Eous,
Et Nouus, atq; alter panditur Auspitijs.

Quilibet punctus magnus continet leucas duode
cim cū dimidia, ita q̃ duo magni puncti continent
viginti quinq; leucas, Cōtinet autē leuca quatuor
Italica miliaria, ita q̃ omnes puncti qui hic cōspi

stone disc, some 3.25 metres (11 feet) in diameter. Archeologists identified the carving as the goddess Coyolxauhqui, 'She who is adorned with bells'. They further concluded that the disc was still in its original position, at the base of the steps to the Templo Mayor. Soon excavation uncovered parts of the grand staircase and the massive stone serpent heads that surrounded the base of the pyramid itself.

Since 1980 the Mexican National Institute of Anthropology and History has conducted a nearly continuous series of excavations and explorations near the Zocalo town square,

site of the Templo Mayor. They have unearthed more than 100 caches of priceless tribute objects that were brought to Tenochtitlan as offerings from conquered regions. The archeological digs have even tunnelled under the streets of Mexico City, in order to make remarkable finds. One of these, known as the House of Eagles, yielded stone and ceramic statues and other treasures. The report of extremely high concentrations of albumin and other bodily substances found on the floors surrounding the statues brings to life the bloody history of the lost city of Tenochtitlan.

Above *This plan of Tenochtitlan was first published in 1524. At the centre of the city is the ritual precinct. This is emphasized by the map, which shows surrounding buildings and natural features as smaller and less important.*

'As has happened in many past civilizations, a new city was simply layered over an ancient one.'

Tenochtitlan

Founded by the Aztecs in 1325, Tenochtitlan was a rich and sophisticated city with a population of more than 200,000, making it one of the largest cities in the world for its time. Its temples, public spaces and marketplaces allowed its elite residents to enjoy comfortable lives. When they marched into the city, the conquistadors of Hernán Cortés were astonished, calling Tenochtitlan one of the finest cities they had ever seen. As empire builders themselves, the Spanish also must have been impressed that Tenochtitlan was the hub of a powerful and far-reaching empire.

The founding of Tenochtitlan fulfilled an ancient prophecy that a wandering people would found a great city when they saw an eagle perched on top of a cactus eating a snake. This signal appeared for the Aztecs on a swampy island on the western side of Lake Texcoco. Although the terrain might have seemed less than ideal, the Aztecs built canals, causeways, dikes and aqueducts to supply water to irrigate farm fields, create habitats for fish and waterfowl and provide fresh water for drinking, bathing and other domestic uses.

Over the years, the Aztecs expanded the site by draining the swamps. At its height, the city covered about 13 square kilometres (5 square miles). It is no wonder that some Spanish chronicles compared it to Venice, another canal city that was the hub of a rich and powerful trading empire. The main features of Tenochtitlan were recorded on a map prepared at the order of Cortés and published in a volume of his letters to the Spanish King Charles V (see page 61).

① AN ISLAND CITY

Around 1450, during the reign of Motecuhzoma I, a dike was constructed to hold back the brackish water of Lake Texcoco and to surround the city with spring-fed fresh water. The fresh water irrigated agricultural fields called *chinampa* (long raised seedbeds between narrow canals).

② CAUSEWAYS AND CANALS

The city was connected to the mainland by causeways. These were interrupted by bridges that allowed canoes to pass freely but could be removed in case of attack. The city itself was interlaced with secondary canals and roadways, so that each of its sections could be reached on foot or by canoe. Four main roads led to the ritual precinct at the centre of the city, three from the causeways and a fourth from a landing place to the east.

③ CALPULLIS

The city's four zones (*campans*) were each divided further into 20 districts (*calpullis*). Within each *calpulli* was a network of smaller canals used for transportation, streets called *tlaxilcallis* and wooden bridges that were removed at night. Competition among the *calpullis* was lively, especially at festival time.

④ MARKETPLACES

Each *calpulli* had its own marketplace and specialized in a particular art or craft, such as the manufacture of pottery, tools, jewellery, figurines, baskets or cloth. There was also a main marketplace where goods brought to the city by traders from cities in the lowlands along the coast were available: tropical bird feathers, jaguar skins, cotton, rubber and cacao beans for chocolate. Trade took place by barter; cacao beans, cotton cloth and lake salt were used as money.

⑤ CEREMONIAL CENTRE

At the centre of the city was a huge walled ceremonial plaza paved with stone. Surrounding the plaza were about 45 public buildings, including the main temples and the palace of the Aztec king. The palace was two storeys high and had more than 100 rooms. Also near the plaza were houses for priests and elite members of the military, schools for training young nobles for the priesthood, a ceremonial ball court and platforms for ritual combat and other religious spectacles. Near by were the homes of Tenochtitlan's elite citizens, many of which featured beautiful gardens, aviaries and zoos.

⑥ TEMPLO MAYOR

Dominating the city was the majestic structure of the Templo Mayor, standing more than 27 metres (90 feet) high. Its twin stepped pyramids rose side by side from a huge platform. The pyramid to the north symbolized the Hill of Sustenance, ruled by Tlaloc, the god of rain. The pyramid to the south represented the Hill of Coatepec and was dedicated to Huitzilopochtli, patron deity of the Aztecs and their god of war.

⑦ SHRINES

Stone shrines at the top of each pyramid temple housed the image of its principal deity. Broad staircases flanked by carved balustrades led up to the shrines. Feathers, bright paper banners and carvings of serpents, frogs and other sacred artwork decorated the exterior of the shrine. Lifelike images of the gods featured ageless faces with open mouths and eyes inlaid with jade and semi-precious stones.

⑧ MOUNTAIN SPRINGS

Two terracotta aqueducts, more than 4 km (2½ miles) long, brought fresh water from the mountain springs. The Spanish said that the people of Tenochtitlan bathed twice each day and that Motecuhzoma bathed four times daily! Many homes had private latrines and small boats collected rubbish and human waste for fertilizer.

CHAPTER 3

CITIES OF HILLS AND MOUNTAINS

Ancient cities of the hills and mountains have a special place in human history. Kings often chose mountain cities as their seat of government because the geography echoed the ruler's elevated status. Some mountain cities were actually citadels – walled fortresses or strongholds to which citizens could retreat in times of attack. Mycenae, with its imposing Lion Gate, was chief among over 300 citadels ruled by warrior-kings in Bronze Age Greece. The earthworks on top of the Hill of Tara are the remains of two ring forts that may have protected the kings and courts of ancient Ireland from attack.

The unique geography of other mountain cities brought prosperity and sometimes calamity to their inhabitants. Petra, carved from living sandstone in a mountain valley, stood at the crossroads of Middle Eastern trade routes. Merchant caravans made the city wealthy. Yet, despite the rich art and lively culture of Pompeii, daily life in the thriving Roman city came to an abrupt and violent end when nearby Mount Vesuvius erupted in 79 CE.

Cities hidden by mists and mountains

Mountain cities often have a special, otherworldly quality. Perhaps this feeling arises from the experience of looking out at the world from a high place. As our vision is drawn towards a distant horizon, the mind and spirit are naturally expanded and refreshed. A high vantage point also gives us a feeling of mastery, of being able to see and thus control the world around us.

It is no wonder, then, that ancient rulers often built their palaces and capital cities on high ground. Mycenae, citadel home of the kings of Greece in the late Bronze Age, offers a view across the Argive Plain to the Saronic Gulf of the Aegean Sea, perhaps encouraging visions of far-flung military campaigns, such as the expedition to Troy. Nemrud Dagi, built by King Antiochus I in the mid-1st century BCE, commands a god-like 360-degree view of the ranges, plains and towns that comprised this ancient kingdom. From the Hill of Tara, Celtic kings in the centuries before the arrival of Christianity could gaze upon a stunning 40 per cent of Ireland. And the spectacular setting of Machu Picchu, at the top of a ridge some 2,135 metres (7,000 feet) above the cloud forest of the Urubamba River canyon, provided a refreshing retreat for the Inca rulers and aristocracy.

A setting in a canyon or mountain valley, on the other hand, can make a city feel secure and protected. Ancient Petra, city of the rocks in what is now Jordan, lies at the end of a narrow gorge that winds its way through towering sandstone cliffs. The canyonside dwellings of the Ancient Pueblo People of the American south-west, such as Cliff Palace at Mesa Verde, were often accessible only by rope or by rock-climbing, giving its inhabitants a sense of security and making their homes easy to defend.

Ironically, the very mountains that protected ancient cities often contributed to their destruction, sometimes in a dramatic way. Pompeii, the elegant Roman city in the shadow of Mount Vesuvius, died in a firestorm when the volcano erupted, and was buried for centuries under tons of pumice and ash.

HIDDEN UTOPIAS

Behind the histories of these actual cities are tales of mythical realms – fantastic utopias hidden from the everyday world. In some traditions these permanently happy lands are equated with otherworldly or heavenly abodes, or with earthly paradises like the Garden of Eden. Stories told of Lyonesse, a vanished domain that once linked Land's End in Cornwall, UK, with the Scilly Isles, are filled with longing for a Golden Age that has perished. The mythical land of Hyperborea, which the ancient Greeks believed lay far to their north, was a perfect place, where the sun shone 24 hours a day.

Part of the allure of paradise lands is that access is difficult. Some are protected by impassable mountains, like the fictional valley of Shangri-La and its mythical Buddhist counterpart Shambhala, which are said to be hidden beyond the Himalayan snow peaks. Others exist in a twilight land, where the veils between the worlds are thin. Arthurian Avalon reputedly lay hidden in the mists that in ancient times swirled around Glastonbury Tor in Somerset. Both Shambhala and Avalon are Realms of the Blessed – what Buddhists call Pure Lands. And both have attracted spiritual adventurers seeking a real-life earthly paradise.

SHANGRI-LA AND SHAMBHALA

Shangri-La is a mystical, harmonious valley that was featured in the 1937 film *Lost Horizon*, directed by Frank Capra, which was based on a novel of the same name by James Hilton. In the film, a group of Western travellers stranded by a plane crash deep in the Himalayas find refuge in a perfect paradise isolated from the outside world by lofty mountains, and guided by wise lamas who live for hundreds of years. The film's hero, British diplomat Robert Conway (played by Ronald Colman), discovers that he has been brought to Shangri-La by the High Lama, who is finally dying and needs someone who is knowledgeable about the modern world to keep the paradise safe.

The fictional Shangri-La is based on an ancient Buddhist myth about Shambhala – a Sanskrit word that has the meaning 'place of peace, happiness and tranquillity'. Shambhala, which like Shangri-La is said to be hidden in the Himalayas, is described as a Pure Land, a society where all the inhabitants are enlightened. Unlike the Pure Lands located in other dimensions, Shambhala is said to be an actual physical place that exists within the human realm. However, only those with impeccably virtuous karma are able to reach it. According to the myth, when the world declines into war and greed, the benevolent king of Shambhala will emerge from his mountain fastness with a huge army to vanquish the corrupt and usher in a worldwide Golden Age.

The daunting spiritual prerequisites to finding Shambhala have not prevented many

real-life travellers from seeking it. Among them was Nicholas Roerich (1874–1947), a Russian-born artist, writer and mystic. Between 1925 and 1928 he led an expedition from India through Tibet, Mongolia and the Altai Mountains of Siberia. Though his announced purpose was to study languages and to paint, Roerich's actual aim was to find Shambhala. A believer in the transcendental unity of all religions, he undertook the journey both as a personal spiritual quest and as an attempt to bring Shambhala to light as a symbol of a coming 'new age' of peace and enlightenment, when all religious divisions will be transcended.

Expeditions with a more sinister goal have also sought Shambhala. Some experts on Nazism and the occult assert that the Nazis sent expeditions to Tibet to find Shambhala and seize its magical powers to help carry out their plan for world domination.

THE MISTS OF AVALON

Distant from Shambhala in terms of geography, but akin in spirit, is the Arthurian paradise known as Avalon. In Celtic mythology, Avalon is a land of eternal summer, an Otherworld that is at the same time the abode of the dead and also a paradise where heroes can be healed of their wounds and live on in eternal youth. In Arthurian romance, Avalon is described as an 'island-valley', a magical abode surrounded by summer seas, where the weather is always fair and orchards and meadows are eternally in bloom. Arthur's great sword Excalibur was forged at Avalon, and it is there that Arthur's half-sister Morgan Le Fay has her magical stronghold. After his final battle, the mortally wounded Arthur is taken to Avalon to be healed, and it is from there that the 'once and future king' will finally return.

Marion Zimmer Bradley's bestselling novel *The Mists of Avalon* (1983) imagines Avalon as a school for druid priestesses headed by Morgaine (Morgan Le Fay), who is fighting to preserve the Celtic traditions threatened by the coming of Christianity. No one who has read the novel, or seen the 2001 television mini-series based on it, can forget the scene in which Morgaine first raises her arms to lift the mists that hide the magical island from view.

Geographically, Avalon is linked with Glastonbury Tor, a conical hill that rises from the flat green meadows of Somerset in the United Kingdom. Though the countryside surrounding the Tor is now dry, in the 5th century (when it is thought that the historical King Arthur lived) the Tor was surrounded by marshland and towered like an island above them. Even today, when mists surround the Tor, it looks like the magical island of British lore.

Like Shambhala, Avalon has a spiritual dimension. The slopes of the Tor appear to be terraced. Many believe that these terraces are the remains of an ancient three-

Left Tibet's spirituality makes it a favoured location for the mysterious domain of Shambhala. The Potala Palace, in the mountain-ringed city of Lhasa, was once the palace of the Dalai Lamas and the spiritual heart of old Tibet.

'So long as people yearn for an end to war and hatred, stories of hidden paradise lands will persist.'

Above *Glastonbury Tor looks particularly magical seen through morning mists. 'Tor' is a Celtic word that means cone-shaped hill. At the top of the Tor is the roofless St Michael's Tower – the remains of a former church.*

dimensional labyrinth. Ascending the labyrinth up the Tor could have been a meditative spiritual practice leading to union with the divine at the summit of the hill. In Christian legend, Joseph of Arimathea brought the Holy Grail to Glastonbury and built Britain's first church at the spot near the Tor where he planted his staff. The staff grew into a thorn tree, the descendant of which is said to still bloom every Christmas.

So long as people yearn for an end to war and hatred, stories about hidden paradise lands will persist. But perhaps the real message of these stories is contained in an old Tibetan parable. In this tale, a young man on a quest for Shambhala crosses the mountains and finally reaches the cave of a hermit. Hearing of his search, the sage admonishes the young man, telling him, 'The kingdom of Shambhala exists only within your own heart.'

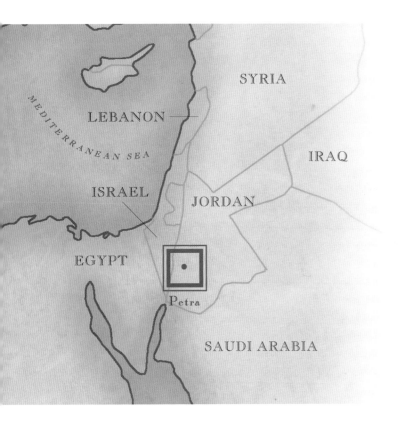

Petra – city of the rocks

Petra – the name means 'rock' in Greek – is famous for its many structures carved from salmon-coloured stone. The city lies in a basin among the mountains of the great valley that runs from the Dead Sea to the Gulf of Aqaba, in what is now Jordan. The Nabataeans, a nomadic tribe of Arabic-speaking Semites, settled in the valley in 312 BCE. Over the next several centuries they carved Petra out of the sandstone to be the capital of their trade empire.

The melding of Egyptian, Greek and Roman architectural styles with the Nabataeans' native design traditions gives the rock city a unique and powerful majesty.

WATER AND ROCKS

Petra is located at the crossroads of several ancient trade routes linking Arabia, Egypt, Damascus and the Mediterranean. Merchant caravans carrying spices and other goods thronged to the city, both because of its strategic location and because of its plentiful supply of water. Although the geography of the city made it prone to flash floods, the Nabataeans engineered a system of dams, cisterns and conduits to divert and contain winter flood waters, assuring the city an ample supply of water even in times of prolonged drought. In effect, Petra was an artificial oasis.

Trade caravans may have approached Petra from the high plateau to the north or across the plain from the south, but the most dramatic approach to the city is from the east. A narrow gorge called the Siq (shaft), in some places only 3–4 metres (10–13 feet) wide, winds through towering sandstone cliffs. At the end of the narrow passageway stands one of Petra's most dramatic building – Al Khazneh, the Treasury, the columns of its Greek façade carved directly from the cliff face. Crusaders occupied Petra towards the end of the city's history, and it is not difficult to imagine that a holy relic was guarded in the Treasury, as depicted in the closing scenes of *Indiana Jones and the Last Crusade*.

SHIFTING ALLEGIANCES

The Nabataeans who built Petra proved remarkably resilient. During the height of their power, in the centuries immediately before and after the birth of Christ, about 20,000 people lived in Petra. When Rome came to power in the region, Petra at first fought off Roman annexation, but then, in 106 BCE, gracefully surrendered and became part of the Roman province of Arabia. The city continued to prosper under Roman rule. Roman builders added to the city's rocky

splendour by constructing a triumphal arch spanning the Siq, a grand colonnaded street, a series of rock tombs and a Roman amphitheatre.

Though an earthquake in 363 CE destroyed half the city, Petra continued to thrive. During the Christian Byzantine period in the 4th century one of the largest rock-cut tombs was converted into a church and Petra became the seat of a Byzantine bishop. However, an even more destructive earthquake rocked the city in 551 CE. With the rise of Islam in the 7th century and alterations in the sea-based trade routes, Petra became a backwater and, except for an 11th-century Crusader castle built near by, was all but forgotten.

REDISCOVERY AND EXCAVATION

Petra was rediscovered in dramatic fashion by Johann Ludwig Burckhardt, a young Anglo-Swiss explorer. While he was on his way from Damascus to Cairo in 1812, Burckhardt heard rumours of an ancient city in the mountains and set off to find it. Disguising himself as an Arab trader who had vowed to sacrifice a goat at the tomb of the Prophet Aaron on a high hill near the city, Burckhardt persuaded two Bedouins to guide him through the Siq until he stood transfixed before the Khazneh. Under the cover of his Arab robes, Burckhardt hastily sketched what he had seen. Other early explorers followed, but systematic work on the site did not begin until the beginning of the 20th century.

Among the recent discoveries are the remains of the Great Temple. Though the structure is in ruins – probably a result of the earthquakes that shook the city – foundation stones and finely carved architectural fragments reveal its art and architecture. Evidence suggests that the temple was built in the last quarter of the 1st century BCE by the Nabataeans, who combined their native traditions with elements of the Classical tradition. Petra's blend of cultures is evident in these remains. A capital decorated with Asian elephant heads, elegantly carved friezes with stone flowers, and fragments of red and white stucco from pillars and walls suggest the building's former glory. Despite 100 years of excavation, archeologists estimate that only 1 per cent of the city has so far been investigated.

'Despite 100 years of excavation, archeologists estimate that only 1 per cent of the city has so far been investigated.'

Opposite The Royal Tombs are carved into a limestone rock face called the King's Wall. Beautiful whorls of coloured sandstone adorn the walls, ceilings and floors of the tomb chambers.

Right Spectacular Al Deir is reached by climbing 800 steps cut into the mountain's rock face. From the 4th century, the site was a monastery for Byzantine monks, who painted crosses on the structure's rear walls.

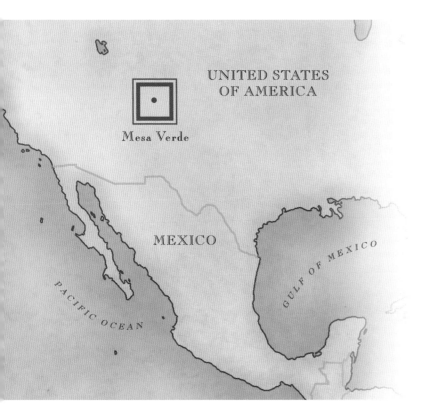

UNITED STATES
OF AMERICA

Mesa Verde

MEXICO

GULF OF MEXICO

PACIFIC OCEAN

Mesa Verde – Cliff Palace of the Ancient Pueblos

Cliff Palace is the largest cliff dwelling in North America. It is built into an alcove in a sandstone cliff in Mesa Verde National Park, in the Four Corners region of the American south-west, where the states of Colorado, Utah, New Mexico and Arizona come together.

The impressive ruin of Cliff Palace was once home to 100–150 Ancient Pueblos, or Anasazi as they are sometimes called. Often accessible only by rope or rock-climbing, these sorts of cliff dwellings provided secure, high-elevation living for the Ancient Pueblos until changing weather patterns, conflicts with neighbouring peoples and social changes caused them to abandon their mountain homes.

LIFE AT CLIFF PALACE

Cliff dwellings developed during the so-called Golden Age of the Ancient Pueblos between 900 and 1130 BCE. During this period the climate of the high mountain mesas was relatively warm and rainfall was adequate. Seep-streams in the region fed by melting winter snows could be diverted to irrigate terraces for garden crops, such as corn, squash and beans. Domesticated

WHY DID CLIFF PALACE COLLAPSE?

Archeologists are far from agreeing why Cliff Palace and other Pueblo settlements were abandoned. The previously accepted theory was that a prolonged period of hotter, drier weather in the late 1200s, called the Great Drought, caused the Ancient Pueblos to migrate to lands further south with more favourable rainfall and dependable streams. Current thinking is that although drought may have made life more difficult for the Pueblo communities, it is more likely that an

increase in territorial warfare – perhaps raids by competing settlements on one another for control of diminishing water resources, food supplies and other necessities – disrupted life in the cliff-dwelling communities.

Other historians suggest that the drought could have caused the cliff dwellers to become disillusioned with their religious practices, many of which were aimed at preserving sufficient rainfall and other favourable ecological conditions. They theorize that the

Ancient Pueblos were drawn south by the new Kachina religion, with its colourful masks and ceremonies. By 1300 CE tens of thousands of Ancient Pueblos had moved to the Hopi mesas (tablelands) of north-eastern Arizona, the Zuni lands of western New Mexico and dozens of adobe villages near the Rio Grande River, merging with existing communities and embracing their religious beliefs.

turkeys were another food source for the inhabitants of the cliff dwellings. Mountains as tall as 3,650 metres (12,000 feet) provided communities with timber, wild game and stone for making flaked tools.

Life in the Pueblo communities was hard, but resources were sufficient to support an expanding population. Communities built literally thousands of small settlements scattered over the region. Technological and social innovations – such as round-bottomed pottery vessels for boiling foods, communal food-sharing and storage, and the use of the bow and arrow for hunting – improved daily living. Craftspeople developed a distinctive style of decorative pottery painted with beautiful red and black geometric designs.

Although there are as many as 600 cliff dwellings of various sizes in the Mesa Verde region, Cliff Palace is the most impressive. This ancient 'apartment complex' measures 88 metres (288 feet) in length and contains approximately 150 rooms. Several multi-storey square and round structures that may have been watchtowers were painted with abstract designs. The 25–30 rooms with hearths were probably living quarters; other spaces were used for food storage.

Perhaps the most interesting areas are the 23 round rooms called *kivas*. Each circular chamber had a central hearth, and a hole in the centre of the roof served as both an entry point and a smoke outlet. Kivas had various ceremonial uses. Some archeologists believe that the central kiva at Cliff Palace was a communal meeting place used to integrate the two different clan groups that occupied the site.

DISCOVERY AND ARCHEOLOGY

Cliff Palace was discovered in December 1888 by two cowboys, Richard Wetherill and Charlie Mason, who were riding across the mesa top looking for stray cattle. Peering through the blowing snow across a vast canyon, they saw something in the cliffs that looked like 'a magnificent city'.

They returned many times over the next years to collect artefacts and guide early explorers and visitors to the site. In 1906, the area surrounding Cliff Palace was protected as a National Park. Soon afterwards Jesse Walter Fewkes of the Smithsonian Institution excavated and stabilized Cliff Palace. The discovery of Cliff Palace began the archeological exploration of the American West. To date, thousands of Ancient Pueblo sites have been identified and explored.

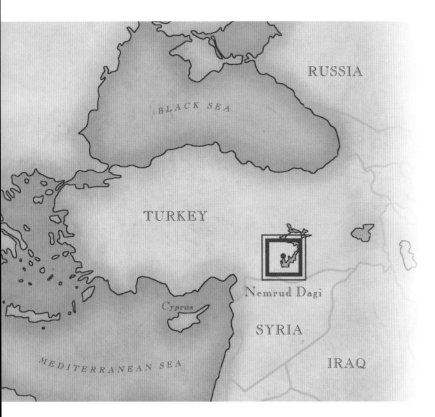

Nemrud Dagi – home of the gods

Set atop one of the highest peaks in the Anti-Taurus Mountains of south-east Turkey is the remarkable city of Nemrud Dagi. At 2,150 metres (7,000 feet) above sea level, this sanctuary, built by King Antiochus I of Commagene in the mid-1st century BCE, lies under snow for nearly half the year.

Forgotten by all but local herders until its rediscovery in 1881, Nemrud Dagi remains a testament to the overweening ambition of one man, Antiochus I, who aspired to the status of a god.

THE COMMAGENE KINGDOM

This ancient kingdom held a strategic position between the Seleucid Empire (the former empire of Alexander the Great) and the Parthian Empire (the empire of ancient Persia). Antiochus' father, Mithridates, was related to the Parthian kings, but he embraced Hellenistic culture and married Laodice, a Seleucid princess. Antiochus continued this tradition of merging East and West and prided himself on his triumphant blending of Greek and Persian religions, culture and traditions into one glorious whole.

Upon gaining the throne in 69 BCE, Antiochus signed a non-aggression treaty with the Romans. The early years of his reign were financially and politically successful, and as the wealth of his kingdom grew, so did the king's ego. He styled himself Antiochus Theos – *Theos* meaning 'God'.

Nemrud Dagi became the chief sanctuary of his ruler cult, and worshippers from all over his kingdom were expected to visit the site on the monthly and yearly anniversary of the king's birth and his accession to the throne.

THE CITY

Nemrud Dagi commanded a 360-degree view of the ranges, plains and towns that comprised Antiochus' ancient kingdom. The site itself consists of three large terraces carved into the mountain to flank its peak at the east, west and north. Worshippers would have made their way to the sanctuary by three processional sacred ways, one leading to each terrace.

The east and west terraces each bear a set of five colossal seated figures measuring 9 metres (30 feet) high. These depict King Antiochus and deities that are a fusion of Greek and Persian gods, such as Apollo-Mithras-Helios and Herakles-Artagnes-Ares. There are dozens of reliefs with larger-than-lifesize figures depicting Antiochus' ancestors and the king being greeted by each member of his pantheon. The site also features altars, temples and the earliest-known calendar horoscope in the form of a striding lion.

The mountain peak itself was covered with rubble chips to create a mound that rose 50 metres (165 feet) above the temple complex. Archeologists have assumed that the tumulus enshrined the remains of Antiochus and have tunnelled extensively into the great cone of rock, searching for his burial site. To date no such site has been found and the purpose of the mound remains a mystery.

REDISCOVERY

The site was first rediscovered by the West when Karl Puchstein, a German engineer, stumbled across the dramatic ruins while surveying the mountain in 1881. Despite his extraordinary reports of colossal sculptures atop the windswept and frequently snow-bound mountain, it was not until 1953 that full-scale excavation of the site began, by an American team led by Theresa Goell. Archeological investigation continues to this day, with many questions remaining to be answered about the significance and meaning of the city.

WHY NEMRUD DAGI WAS LOST

The remote mountain location of the sanctuary preserved its mystery for centuries after Nemrud's collapse, but why did the sanctuary fall into ruin so quickly? We know that Antiochus' apparently astute treaties with the Romans, the dominant power of the day, ultimately came to nothing. The Commagene rulers who followed Antiochus sided with Mark Antony in the Roman civil war, only to fall out of favour when Antony was defeated by Augustus and the balance of power in the Roman world shifted. Antiochus' Commagene kingdom was made a Roman client-state and continued as such until 72 CE, when it was fully incorporated into the Roman Empire.

And what of the wanton destruction of the site itself? Who or what caused it? According to some reports, it was the Romans who toppled the colossal statues, while other sources suggest that the earthquakes that plague the area were responsible.

Ultimately it seems that Antiochus' hubris in believing that Nemrud Dagi would be a 'home of the gods', and the city a spiritual centre for the Middle East, was punished by both humans and nature. His ambition was to achieve a unique synthesis of Greek and Persian religion and culture embodied in his own divine person. Yet Antiochus proved to be an insignificant ruler of a minor kingdom that was no match for the might of the dominant world power of his day. Today his toppled head lies atop a windswept mountain, a refuge for stray sheep, goats and an eyrie for birds of prey.

ECUADOR

BRAZIL

PERU

PACIFIC OCEAN

Machu Picchu

BOLIVIA

CHILE

Machu Picchu – royal citadel of the Incas

Machu Picchu is a spectacular Incan citadel perched on the summit of the Old Peak (Machu Picchu) in Peru's Andes. Its setting beneath the granite peak of Huayna Picchu (Young Peak), which towers 185 metres (600 feet) to the north, is as much a part of the site's beauty and mystery as its ruins. There are around 200 buildings, about half of which had religious significance.

Left *The uneven, mountainous terrain of Machu Picchu was transformed through the use of terraces and flights of stone steps. Terracing provided level space for agriculture and for dwellings, blending human needs with the natural surroundings.*

WHY WAS MACHU PICCHU DESERTED?

As there is no reference to Machu Picchu in the chronicles of the conquistadors, it seems that it was never found by the Spanish. In fact, archeologists believe that the citadel had been all but abandoned before the Spanish arrived.

Several theories have been proposed that seek to explain why Machu Picchu was deserted. One holds that a war between rival Incan tribes led to their extermination. Others theorize that an epidemic (perhaps smallpox or syphilis) killed off the population. But the most likely explanation is that with the decline of the Inca ruling class, Machu Picchu lost its reason for existing. Before the arrival of the Spanish in 1531, the Inca Empire stretched for more than 3,680 km (2,300 miles) along the Andes peaks. Incan rulers, travelling along a network of well-constructed roads and trails, probably spent part of the year in a number of royal estates. In season, it is likely that Machu Picchu was home to 500–750 people – the ruling Incas and their servants, priests and craftspeople.

With the decline of the Inca Empire and the decimation of the ruling class, Machu Picchu became irrelevant and was soon abandoned and reclaimed by the jungle.

Built between 1450 and 1470 CE by Inca emperor Pachacuti as a royal retreat, the construction of Machu Picchu on a ridge 2,135 metres (7,000 feet) above the Urubamba River, and 113 km (70 miles) north-west of the Inca capital of Cuzco, was a stupendous achievement. Since the master builders did not use the wheel, huge blocks of stone were cut, moved and placed with bronze and stone tools, inclined planes and human effort. Although the blocks are of different sizes and have many faces, they fit together perfectly without the use of mortar, with joints so tight that even the thinnest knife blade cannot fit between them.

SACRED AND SECULAR

Outside the city, farmers grew maize and potatoes on terraces irrigated by a system of cisterns and stone channels. The workshops of potters, stonemasons and weavers were located inside the urban section, along with stone houses with steep thatched roofs for servants and craftspeople. In this area there was also a more refined grouping of houses built of reddish stone for the Amautas, high-ranking teachers and intellectuals.

Divided from the urban section by a central plaza is the sacred section, which contains the grand buildings erected for the Inca royalty, who used the city as a place to relax, hunt and entertain dignitaries. Many of the structures had a spiritual aspect. For example, the Intihuatana or 'sun's hitching post', is a column of stone sited on top of a hill so that its corners point to the four compass directions. Astrological observatory and ritual altar, the Intihuatana was the focus of ceremonies at the time of the winter solstice. As the nights drew in, a priest would perform a ceremony to tie the sun to the post and prevent it from disappearing.

DRAMATIC REDISCOVERY

In 1911 Hiram Bingham (a lecturer in Latin American history at Yale University in New Haven, Connecticut, and a real-life Indiana Jones) set out into the Andes hoping to find clues to the fate of the Incas. After weeks of arduous trekking in search of Vilcabamba, the still-undiscovered last stronghold of the Incas, Bingham – on the advice of a local peasant – crawled through thickets up a snake-infested mountainside until he reached the walls of houses of the 'finest quality of Inca stone work', which, he wrote, 'fairly took my breath away'.

He returned to the site in 1912 and 1914 to clear away the jungle and reveal the full glory of Machu Picchu to the modern world. The article he wrote describing his discovery, published in *Harper's Monthly* magazine in 1913, and his bestselling book *The Lost City of the Incas* (1948), captured the public imagination. Unfortunately, Bingham's conclusions about the site have mainly proved incorrect. However, the extensive collection of artefacts he brought back from the site, including pottery, copper and bronze jewellery and intricately carved knives, has provided scholars with material for years of further study.

Below *Buildings at Machu Picchu feature polished dry-stone walls of regular shape. Incan builders were masters of the ashlar technique, in which blocks of stone were cut to fit together tightly without mortar.*

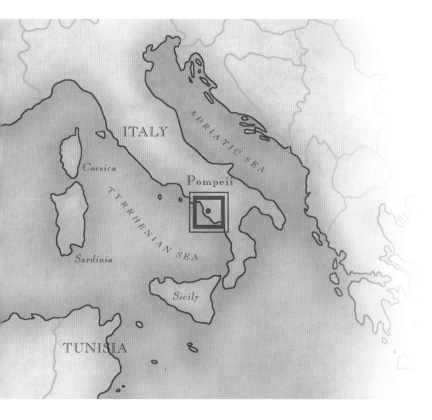

Pompeii – in the shadow of Mount Vesuvius

On 24 August 79 CE, the Roman city of Pompeii, near modern Naples, was destroyed by an eruption of Mount Vesuvius, about 8 km (5 miles) to the north-east. Buried under pumice and ash, Pompeii was lost for about 1,700 years but has now been extensively studied.

Many of Pompeii's private houses and public buildings, filled with artefacts and artworks, were preserved for posterity by the ash fall that smothered the city. This has offered historians and visitors a unique opportunity to walk backwards in time.

ROMAN POMPEII

Archeologists believe that Pompeii was founded in the 6th century BCE by the Osci, a people of central Italy. After it became a Roman colony in 89 BCE, Pompeii experienced some extensive development, including the construction of a new amphitheatre, a central *natatorium* or swimming pool and an aqueduct that supplied water to public baths and fountains, as well as to the private homes. During the 1st century, between 12,000 and 20,000 people lived in Pompeii, including many Roman officials who built luxurious holiday villas in and near the city.

Pompeii's buildings were often beautifully decorated with statues, wall paintings and elaborate mosaics. Some of the artworks depict historical events, such as the victory of Alexander the Great over the Persian King Darius. Others represent Greek gods and stories from myth, such as Venus on a seashell. Many of the artworks have a sexual theme, including wall paintings on a brothel that may have been early advertisements.

Left Among the many excavated shops are 33 bakeries, such as this one on the Via Consolare. Some wood-burning ovens were found to contain the carbonized remains of loaves of bread that were being baked at the time of the eruption.

When they were first discovered, many erotic artworks were hidden out of prudery; some became available for general viewing only in 2000.

THE VOLCANO ERUPTS

Historians know a great deal about what happened during the destruction of Pompeii because of an extraordinary eye-witness account composed by Pliny the Younger. In 79 CE, Pliny the Elder, the Roman soldier, writer and naturalist, was commanding a fleet stationed near Pompeii. After watching the beginnings of the eruption from afar, he travelled closer with his nephew Pliny the Younger to get a better view. Caught in the ash fall, Pliny the Elder was overcome by fumes and died. His nephew later described the first few hours of the eruption and his uncle's death in two letters to the Roman historian Tacitus.

Modern vulcanologists and archeologists have used Pliny's letters, along with the study of exposed volcanic rock in the Bay of Naples, to understand what happened. As they now believe, Pompeii had suffered extensive damage from a violent earthquake in 62 CE. Seventeen years later parts of the city were still being reconstructed. On 20 August 79 CE and for the next four days, new quakes shook the city and streams near the volcano dried up.

Then, shortly after noon on 24 August, Vesuvius exploded. Pliny the Younger wrote that an enormous cloud of ash and rock was thrown into the air, blocking out the sun. Experts think most people survived this fall of pumice and ash, but were killed shortly after midnight by the searing heat of 'pyroclastic surges' – streams of poisonous gas and ash that rushed from the cone at more than 100 km (60 miles) an hour.

ROYAL TREASURE HUNT

In March 1748 a surveying engineer was sent by Bourbon King Charles III to supply his court in Naples with antiquities. The engineer inspected a water channel that had been dug 150 years earlier through the site of Pompeii. When he returned to court with evidence that there were indeed antiquities at the site, a royal treasure hunt began, during which many frescoes and mosaics were stripped from the site and removed to Naples, where they remain to this day on display in the Museo Nazionale.

In the 19th century, during the period when the French had control of Naples, excavation became better organized. By 1860 much of western Pompeii had been uncovered and this is where most of the impressive and intact Roman ruins are still located. From 1863 to 1875 the excavation was directed by the Italian archeologist Giuseppe Fiorelli, whose technique of excavating buried houses from the top down yielded Pompeii's most dramatic artefacts.

'Excavation has revealed a lively snapshot of Roman life in the 1st century, frozen at a moment in time.'

By injecting plaster into voids that he encountered within the ash layer, he created accurate and eerie casts of Pompeii's dead, often with their final expressions of terror clearly visible.

Though about one-third of the city still remains buried, current archeological work is aimed at restoring and preserving previously investigated masonry and frescoes that are now deteriorating after two centuries of exposure.

Above This wall painting, which adorned a tavern on Pompeii's Via di Mercurio, shows two men sitting at a wooden table playing a game of dice, while two other men look on.

Pompeii

Much of our contemporary understanding of the daily lives of ancient Romans derives from the treasures of art and architecture that have been uncovered at Pompeii and the nearby city of Herculaneum, which was also destroyed by the eruption of Vesuvius in 79 CE. Historians have learned as much from the excavation of the shops, workshops, public toilets and modest houses of Pompeii as they have from the lavish villas decorated with mosaics and other artwork.

The topography of Pompeii is typically Roman: straight streets in a regular grid with right-angled intersections and houses and shops lining both sides of the road. The Via dell'Abbondanza, lined with inns, was one of the most important thoroughfares.

Pompeii's largest private house was the House of the Faun. Named for the bronze statuette of a faun found there, it belonged to the wealthy patrician Casii. The villa has a mosaic threshold, two interior gardens surrounded by porticoes and a central structure with Corinthian columns topped with painted capitals. In one room is a giant mosaic of Alexander the Great composed of about one million tesserae.

The best-preserved residence in Pompeii, the House of the Vetti, belonged to a pair of wealthy brothers, whose signet rings were discovered during excavation. The Vetti may have been wine merchants. An ornate and formal garden was filled with marble and bronze statues, including 12 fountainheads that spouted water into basins. The garden was surrounded by an elaborately decorated portico, with entrances to rooms that were used for business and entertaining.

① FORUM

Like all Roman cities, Pompeii had its bustling Forum. This contained the city's main religious, commercial and civic structures, including the Sacrarium of the Lares (a building that housed the town's guardian deities), the Macellum (see below) and the Basilica (Pompeii's largest building, used for legal and commercial business).

② GREAT TEMPLE OF JUPITER

At the northern side of the Forum is the Great Temple of Jupiter. Built in 150 BCE, it became Pompeii's main temple when the city fell under the Roman Republic's rule. Inside the temple lay the *cella*, accessible only to the priests, which contained at its far end three niches occupied by statues of Juno, Jupiter and Minerva.

③ MACELLUM

At the north-east corner of the Forum is the Macellum (Latin for 'market'), a courtyard where food was sold, especially meat and fish. The courtyard has three gates and is fronted by a portico with two kiosks for money-changers. The walls are decorated with frescoes including images of birds, fish and pottery vessels. The remains of fish bones and scales have been found in the drains. Archeologists believe that the Macellum was rebuilt several times over the centuries and that at the time of the eruption reconstruction was again underway.

④ BUILDING OF EUMACHIA

Near the Forum is a building named for Eumachia, a priestess and patroness of the Guild of Fullers, the city's most influential guild. Fullers were clothing makers, dyers and cleaners and this building probably served as their headquarters. On the base of a statue of Eumachia now in the Museo Nazionale in Naples is this inscription: 'To Eumachia, daughter of Lucius, public priestess, the fullers [dedicated this statue]'.

⑤ TEMPLE OF APOLLO

Close to the Forum, but much older, is a temple to Apollo, parts of which have been dated to the 6th century BCE. The temple's perimeter is surrounded by 48 columns. A long flight of steps leads to the inner sanctuary or *cella*. The main altar was adorned with statues of Apollo and of his twin sister, moon goddess Diana. Apollo's association with the sun is indicated by a sundial on one of the columns surrounding the *cella*.

⑥ VILLA OF THE MYSTERIES

Sited about 800 metres (½ mile) north-west of the main part of Pompeii, this villa contained a wine-press and fine rooms for dining and entertaining. It is named for the frescoes that line the walls of a room known as the Initiation Chamber. There are several interpretations of these images, but the generally accepted theory is that they depict scenes of the initiation of a woman to the secret cult of Dionysus, perhaps as a rite of passage into adulthood or as a preparation for her marriage.

⑦ VESUVIUS

Situated about 9 km (6 miles) east of Naples, Mount Vesuvius is the only volcano in mainland Europe to have erupted within the last 100 years. It is regarded as one of the most dangerous volcanoes in the world because more than 3 million people live near by. The ancient Greeks and Romans considered the mountain sacred to the hero-god Hercules. Named for Hercules, the ancient town of Herculaneum at the mountain's base was also destroyed in the eruption of 79 CE that buried Pompeii.

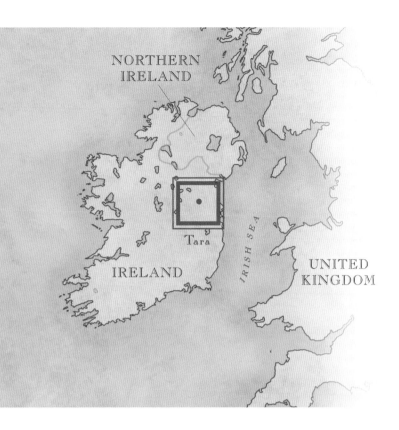

NORTHERN
IRELAND

Tara

IRELAND

IRISH SEA

UNITED
KINGDOM

Tara – hilltop capital of ancient Ireland

Rising gently from the emerald pastures of County Meath in Leinster, 48 km (30 miles) north-west of Dublin, and commanding a stunning view of 40 per cent of Ireland, is the limestone ridge known as the Hill of Tara. The site's ancient monuments, some dating back to the Neolithic period, recall a time when Tara was the capital of pre-Christian Ireland.

Whether the Celtic High King ruled Ireland from Tara is unclear, but a standing stone within the hill fort at the top of the ridge is believed to be the Lia Fáil – the Stone of Destiny – at which the Celtic High Kings were crowned.

MOUND OF THE HOSTAGES

The oldest structure on the Hill of Tara is a Neolithic passage tomb called the Mound of the Hostages, which gets its name from the custom of Irish kings holding hostages from all the provinces of Ireland to ensure their loyalty. The tomb has a short passage that is aligned with sunset on the astronomical cross-quarter days of 8 November and 4 February – the original dates of the ancient Celtic festivals of Samhain and Imbolc.

The mound was excavated in the 1950s by Sean P. O'Riordain and Ruaidhri de Valera, both archeologists from University College Dublin. They discovered a rich collection of Neolithic and early Bronze Age burials and artefacts, which included decorative beads, pendants, bone and antler pins, bronze daggers, a ceremonial stone battleaxe, food vessels and urns. The finds, which were kept

in storage for nearly 50 years, have recently been studied using contemporary methods by Dr Muiris O'Sullivan, head of UCD's School of Archaeology. Radiocarbon analysis carried out on bone fragments found in the tomb has confirmed that the site dates to around 3500 BCE and suggests that the Hill of Tara was important long before the arrival of the Celts.

Though ancient Irish history is often intertwined with myth, many believe that Tara was the site of the capital city of the Firbolg, one of the early races to inhabit Ireland. Later it was the seat of the Tuatha de Danaan, the mythical race considered to be the ancestors of Celtic fairy folk; and of the Milesians (also known as the Gaels), who arrived in Ireland about 1500 BCE.

CAPITAL OF CELTIC KINGS

Although only a series of circular earthwork enclosures are visible today and no buildings remain on the site, Celtic myth supplies other details. It is said that each of the provincial Celtic kings had a house set aside for him on Tara, where he resided during meetings of the Parliament. Meetings were

TARA: A SPANISH CONNECTION?

According to legend, Erimhon, an ancient Celtic king, travelled to Spain where he fell in love with a beautiful woman named Tea. He enticed her back to his native land and, as a wedding present, gave her the most beautiful hill in Ireland, which he named after her. Whether or not this story accounts for the name of the hill, following the arrival of the Celts in about 500 BCE, Tara was associated with Celtic royalty.

'The Hill of Tara was important long before the arrival of the Celts.'

held in the Great Banqueting Hall, a long, narrow rectangular feature to the north of the hill. Though archeologists now believe that the Banqueting Hall is more likely to have been a ceremonial avenue that approached the site, Celtic enthusiasts populate it with an assembly of kings, chiefs, nobles, historians and bards. In ancient times, they say, five great roads radiated out from Tara to all parts of the country.

Also according to legend, the Lia Fáil, the standing stone at the centre of the earthwork ring known as the Royal Seat, would roar three times if the chosen man was, in fact, the true High King. High Kings

were crowned at the stone until at least the 6th century.

Tara is also associated with stories about the confrontation between Christianity and paganism. According to legend, St Patrick lit the Easter fire on Slane – a hill at the opposite end of the valley from Tara – in defiance of King Loegaire, who was meeting his druid priests on Tara. This challenge created first indignation, then respect in the court of the High King. Soon Tara became Patrick's headquarters, from which he began converting the Irish to Christianity. A grave found near Tara is said to be that of King Loegaire, the last pagan king of Ireland.

Above *A number of large earthworks survive on the Hill of Tara. In the centre of the hill fort, an Iron Age enclosure, are two linked ring forts. The one to the east is called Cormac's House; the one to the west, The Royal Seat.*

Mycenae – Greek citadel stronghold

Mycenae was the capital of a late Bronze Age state that dominated the eastern Mediterranean and southern Greece from 1600 to 1100 BCE. From the royal palace on its citadel hill, Mycenaean kings could look across the Argive Plain to the Saronic Gulf of the Aegean. From there, Greek soldiers sailed off to the Trojan War under Mycenae's legendary warrior-king, Agamemnon.

Agamemnon's deeds, and those of the House of Atreus (his extended family), have been celebrated by poets, playwrights and artists from the days of Homer and Aeschylus until today.

MYCENAEAN GREECE

Archeologists can reconstruct much about life at Mycenae from tablets written in a script called Linear B, an early form of Greek. The tablets record that the sole holder of power in Mycenaean culture was the king. He functioned as the chief priest, the commander of the military and the supreme judge. Wealth in the form of gold, silver and bronze objects, stores of grain and animal herds were also controlled and allocated according to the king's wishes.

The king was surrounded by a hierarchy of court officials, warriors, priests and scribes. Officials of these groups also lived in the citadel, making the culture highly centralized. The warriors supported the power of the king by controlling access to the territory he ruled. Scribes recorded taxes and kept track of the complex details of trades, tributes and other transactions.

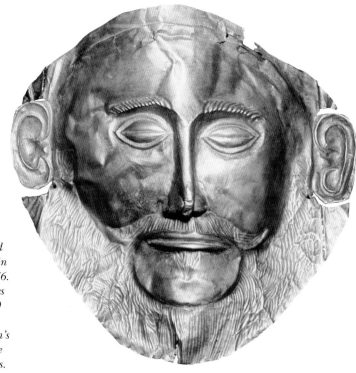

Right The Mask of Agamemnon is a gold funeral mask found in a burial shaft in 1876. Current research dates the mask to some 400 years earlier than the dates for Agamemnon's rule. Nevertheless, the popular name persists.

Priests performed rituals and divined the future at the king's request.

For over 300 years, Mycenaean culture dominated the Greek mainland. By 1500 BCE, Greece was dotted with at least 320 citadels whose lords controlled fiefdoms of villages and estates. The King of Mycenae was the most important of these rulers, and all of the citadels paid allegiance to him. This political structure was echoed in the Greek pantheon,

Left *The main gate to the citadel of Mycenae is topped by a carving of two lions flanking a pillar. The carved stone, which weighs less than the stones to the right and left, is called a 'relieving triangle' as it reduces pressure on the lintel stone over the doorway.*

in which lesser gods, even Poseidon, the ruler of the seas, and Athena, goddess of wisdom and champion of heroes, paid allegiance to Zeus, the king of the gods.

DECLINE AND DESTRUCTION

No record remains of the social and political changes that led to the fall of Mycenae and of Mycenaean culture as a whole. What is known is that by 1100 BCE the era of Mycenaean dominance had come to an end. An increase in population, the distant military campaigns such as the conquest of Troy and migrations into Greece by Dorian-speaking people from the north probably all contributed to weakening the king's absolute power. Many Greek citadels were burned or razed, including the one at Mycenae. Once-royal Mycenae was reduced to a minor town, as all of Greece slipped into a Dark Age that lasted 300 years.

ARCHEOLOGY AND TREASURES

The excavation of Mycenae began with wealthy German businessman Heinrich Schliemann (1822–1890). Fascinated by Homer's accounts of the Trojan War, he set out to find the sites that Homer described. After his rediscovery of Troy, Schliemann turned his attention to Mycenae.

In 1876, in a ring of shaft graves located inside Mycenae's main gate, Schliemann discovered the richest treasure in the history of Greek archeology. The trove included gold cups and crowns, inlaid swords and five gold burial masks, one of which Schliemann called the death mask of Agamemnon. It stars with other treasures from Mycenae in an exhibit at the National Archeological Museum of Athens.

Discoveries continue to be made at Mycenae. In 1958 rooms were excavated along the south wall that clearly had a religious or cult purpose. Their meaning is still being studied. The written language of Mycenae, Linear B, was not deciphered until 1953. Tablets written in the script are still being found and read today. Perhaps one will shed light on the collapse of the Mycenaean culture.

'The treasure trove included gold cups and crowns, inlaid swords and five gold burial masks.'

Mycenae

Mycenae lies in the far north of the Argive Plain on the Peloponnese, the large peninsula that makes up the southern part of the Greek mainland. Judging from pottery shards, archeologists believe that the site has been occupied since about 3500 BCE. The citadel reconstructed here dates from the late Bronze Age, about 1600–1100 BCE, the time of Agamemnon and the mythological Trojan War.

Greek myth and a cycle of plays called *The Oresteia* by Aeschylus (*c.* 525–465 BCE) tells of the tragedy that befell the House of Atreus, the dynasty of Agamemnon, King of Mycenae. As the story goes, in order to gain favourable winds for his journey to Troy, Agamemnon, the leader of the Greek forces, sacrifices his daughter Iphigenia. While he is away at Troy, Agamemnon's wife Clytemnestra, furious over the murder of her daughter, takes Aegisthus as her lover.

After ten years of war, Agamemnon sails home to Mycenae. A string of signal fires in the mountains announce his arrival. Clytemnestra greets her husband and leads him to a warm bath. There he is murdered by his wife and her lover, Aegisthus, who seizes the throne of Mycenae for himself.

In the final acts, Agamemnon's son Orestes returns to Mycenae. Orestes kills his mother and her lover, after which he is driven out of Mycenae and pursued by the avenging Furies of guilt until he is absolved of his crime by the goddess Athena.

Ironically, soon after the death of Agamemnon, Mycenae and the other citadels of Greece's Bronze Age culture were burned and abandoned as centres of power. By 200 CE, when the Greek geographer Pausanias travelled through the area, Mycenae was a ruin.

① CYCLOPAEAN WALLS

The massive walls of the citadel of Mycenae announce the city's importance. In thickness, the outer walls average 6 metres (20 feet), but they were once probably much higher than is shown by present remains, perhaps averaging 12 metres (40 feet). They are built in a style called 'cyclopaean' because the blocks of stone are so massive it was thought in later times that only giants, like the one-eyed Cyclops, could have moved them. Around 1250 BCE, the city's walls were extended to bring Grave Circle A within the fortress, perhaps an indication of the importance of the graveyard and its contents.

② THE LION GATE

Still standing today, the entrance gate to the citadel of Mycenae is an imposing sight. The triangular sculpture above the lintel features two realistically carved lions. The heads of the lions were originally carved from a softer material such as metal or soapstone that has long since disappeared. The column between the lions is a motif from Minoan culture that represents the Goddess.

③ GRAVE CIRCLE A

Uncovered by Heinrich Schliemann in 1876, this circle contains shaft graves that yielded the richest treasure ever found in Greek archeology. Though Schliemann believed that the gold grave masks and other treasures belonged to Agamemnon, later work has revealed that the last burial in the circle took place centuries earlier. The riches found in the graves show a similarity between Mycaenean burial practices and those of ancient Egypt.

④ THE GREAT RAMP

Extending from the Lion Gate and running beside the grave circle is the sacred processional avenue that connects the gates with the palace and the shrine.

⑤ HILLTOP PALACE

The hilltop placement of the royal palace located the king physically above his lands and people. No one but the king, his household and high officials lived on the citadel.

⑥ THE MEGARON

The central room of the palace is the Megaron. The room was dominated by a central circular hearth, above which a roof opening let smoke escape. Fragments of frescoes can still be seen on the northern wall. The king's throne stood at the centre of the south wall. Tables for food and wine served in gold and silver vessels were carried in at need. The king's private quarters were above the Megaron, with a private bath and open court.

⑦ THE ARCHAIC TEMPLE OF ATHENA

On the summit of the citadel, near the palace, was the site of the later Temple of Athena, erected during the 6th century BCE. The temple featured Doric columns and was aligned with the rising of the Pleiades, the star cluster that rises in the east with the sun to mark Athena's feast day. The King of Mycenae functioned as the chief priest of the shrine.

CHAPTER 4
CITIES OF JUNGLES AND FORESTS

Hidden in the dense foliage of the jungles and forests of the Americas, Africa and South-East Asia are lost cities that have enticed explorers, treasure-seekers and conquerors for centuries. The great cities of Copán, Tikal and Palenque served as administrative and ceremonial centres at the height of the Mayan civilization. The jungles of Latin America also conceal fabled or mythical lost cities, such as Eldorado, Ciudad Blanca and the City of Z – all of which have been sought unsuccessfully by those drawn by the lure of treasure.

Forests and jungles are also the setting for the capitals of ancient empires. Cahokia in the woodlands of the Mississippi River valley was the largest Native American city north of Meso-America. In Africa, Great Zimbabwe was the heart of a trading kingdom founded by the Shona people, well known to Arab and European traders around 350 CE.

Tales of rediscovery, adventure and madness

The ruins of ancient cities lost in the foliage of jungles and rainforests have always attracted the interest of adventurers and treasure-seekers. In many instances the lure that draws adventurers to scale mountains covered with cloud forest, paddle down uncharted jungle rivers or hack with machetes into rainforests is gold. Though to Europeans gold signifies money and riches, to many indigenous peoples gold was a sacred metal that symbolized the power of the sun, fertility and life. Christopher Columbus viewed it in more spiritual terms: 'Gold is the most exquisite of all things . . . with gold he [who possesses it] can gain entrance for his soul into paradise.'

Columbus' 'discovery' of the American continents in 1492 launched an invading army of European explorers and conquerors into the forests and jungles of the 'New World' in search of riches.

Though the great Mayan city-states of Copán, Tikal and Palenque had already been reclaimed by the rainforest before the arrival of the Spanish conquistadors, their central Mexican successor, the gold-filled Aztec city of Tenochtitlan (see pages 60–63), fell to Hernán Cortés in 1521. Less than five years later, his desire for treasure still unsatisfied, Cortés searched unsuccessfully through the jungles of Honduras for the legendary Ciudad Blanca – the White City – which he believed had wealth to rival Tenochtitlan. Gold also lured explorers into the jungles of Africa. European and Arab traders first visited the African markets of Great Zimbabwe in search of Ophir, the city mentioned in the Bible as the source of the gold that the Queen of Sheba supplied to embellish the Temple of Solomon.

Following the gold-seekers into jungles and forests came missionaries in search of souls to save. In 1695 Franciscan monk Antonio de Avendano was the first European to visit the ruins of the Mayan city of Tikal. And the massive earthen mounds of Cahokia in the woodlands of North America's Mississippi Valley were rediscovered by French missionary monks, who named the largest mound after themselves.

In the 20th century adventurers and archeologist-explorers were still being lured into the jungle by dreams of treasure and fame. In 1939 American explorer Theodore Morde spent five months cutting through dense vegetation and navigating miles of uncharted waterways on the Mosquito Coast of Honduras in search of Ciudad Blanca. And in 1993 archeologists following in the footsteps of Hiram Bingham (celebrated for his rediscovery of Machu Picchu, see pages 76–77) used high-tech images to guide their search for Llactapata, another lost Incan city.

THE LEGEND OF ELDORADO
Behind the search for these actual lost cities is a myth that has stirred the imagination of explorers and adventurers for hundreds of years. Eldorado – the legendary city of gold believed to be hidden somewhere in South America – has persisted as a symbol of instant riches since the early 1600s. The name Eldorado (or *El Dorado*, meaning 'the gilded one' in Spanish) refers at the same time both to a golden man or golden king and to his lost city.

The legend can be traced back to rumours heard by Spanish conquistadors in 1539 when they encountered the Muisca people in what is now Colombia. According to these stories, a ceremony to recognize the lordship of a new king used to take place among the people living at Lake Guatavita, near Bogotá. In 1636 Spanish chronicler Juan Rodriquez Freyle wrote an account of this ceremony based on what he said were eye-witness reports: after a period of seclusion, the new king would sail a raft out into Lake Guatavita to make offerings to the powerful spirit who lived at the bottom of the lake. Before setting forth, the king's bare skin would be covered with sticky resin and coated with gold dust blown through a pipe. The raft on which El Dorado, the Golden Man, travelled was laden with treasure – heaps of gold, emeralds, bracelets, pendants, earrings, crowns and other riches. At a given signal, El Dorado would throw the golden treasure into the centre of the lake.

Over the years, many adventurers tried to recover the vast treasure thought to lie at the bottom of Lake Guatavita. The most serious early attempt took place in the 1580s when Antonio de Sepulveda, a Bogotá merchant, employed 8,000 Native American workers to cut a notch in the rim of the lake to lower its water level. Though the plan succeeded in lowering the water by 20 metres (65 feet), revealing priceless treasures, the notched

hillsides soon collapsed, killing many workers. Among the riches recovered from the lake were a golden breastplate and an emerald the size of a hen's egg! They were sent to King Philip of Spain.

In 1911 an English gold company did succeed in draining Lake Guatavita by means of tunnels and sluices. But the muddy lake bottom quickly hardened and the lake refilled with rainwater. The company was forced to auction off the few gold objects it had recovered to pay its debts.

THE SEARCH FOR ELDORADO
The legend of El Dorado soon became attached to speculation about a lost city of

Above *In 1595, Sir Walter Raleigh led an expedition to what is now Guyana. This woodcut, showing how noble visitors were groomed, was an illustration in the book he wrote afterwards.*

'Eldorado – the legendary city of gold said to be somewhere in South America – has persisted as a symbol of instant riches since the early 1600s.'

gold – a place where people were reputed to cook in golden pots and eat from golden plates. This fabulous city, which was also called Eldorado, was thought to be hidden somewhere deep within the rainforests of the Amazon basin. Over the next centuries many expeditions were mounted to search for the site.

In February 1541 Spanish conquistadors Francisco de Orellana and Gonzalo Pizarro led an expedition eastwards from Quito in Ecuador. After following the Coca and Napo Rivers deep into the rainforest, the expedition force of 4,000-plus Spaniards and Native Americans started to run out of provisions. More than 3,000 people died. It was decided that Orellana would continue sailing down the Napo River with a small force in search of food while Pizarro, who believed the expedition had failed, returned with another group of survivors to Quito. Though Orellana did not find Eldorado, he

Above Lake Guatavita, in today's Colombia, was sacred to the Muisca people, whose ceremonies gave birth to the legend of El Dorado. The notch in the cliff side is evidence of an attempt by the Spanish Conquistadors to drain the lake and recover its treasures.

is credited with being the first European to sail the length of the Amazon River, arriving at its mouth in August 1542.

In 1595 the poet and adventurer Sir Walter Raleigh, a favourite of Queen Elizabeth I, sailed 640 km (400 miles) down the Orinoco, South America's third-largest river. He suffered from hunger, sickness and attacks by poisoned arrows, but did not find Eldorado. When his second expedition in search of the golden city went disastrously wrong in 1618, the failure was used by England's King James as a pretext for Raleigh's execution.

THE LOST CITY OF Z

Closely related to the Eldorado myth is the continuing mystery of what happened to Colonel Percy Fawcett, a British adventurer who disappeared in the jungles of Brazil in 1925. Fawcett first visited South America in 1906, when he was sent to map the border between Bolivia and Brazil on behalf of the Royal Geographical Society. Fawcett returned to the area seven times between 1906 and 1924 to pursue his interest in local wildlife and archeology.

Sometime during this period Fawcett became convinced that a fabulous city of gold, which he called the City of Z, lay hidden somewhere in the southern basin of the Amazon River, between the Talajós and Xingu tributaries. As evidence for this belief, Fawcett cited carvings he had seen on rocks and documents from Portuguese conquistadors, which he had found in Brazilian archives.

In 1925 Fawcett travelled to Brazil, with his son Jack and a friend of his son, to search for the lost city. On 25 May 1925 he sent a last telegram to his wife and disappeared. More than 13 subsequent expeditions have retraced Fawcett's route attempting to learn his fate, and more than 100 other explorers have died or failed to return.

Was Fawcett killed by the Kalapalo, an indigenous people of the area, as some authorities have claimed? Did he die of a tropical disease, starve to death or was he eaten by jaguars? Or, as has recently been proposed, is the truth even stranger?

Previously unpublished letters that have now come to light suggest that Fawcett had no intention of ever returning to Britain. Under the influence of a native female 'spirit guide', he may have planned to 'go native' and set up a commune in the jungle based on a bizarre blend of beliefs that included worship of his own son Jack and the tenets of Theosophy, a philosophy that emphasizes revelations of the eternal truths at the root of all religions.

Whatever happened to Fawcett, his fate – and the location of the fabulous lost city of Eldorado and the City of Z – continues to lure adventurers to the jungles and forests of South America. New expeditions to pursue the latest clues to Fawcett's fate are currently being planned.

Left British adventurer Colonel Percy Fawcett, shown here before his ill-fated 1925 expedition into the jungles of South America in search of the mythical gold-filled City of Z.

Copán – Classic-period Mayan splendour

The great Mayan city-states of what are now Mexico, Guatemala and Honduras comprise one of the major lost civilizations of the world. Hundreds of cities and towns were hidden for centuries under a dense canopy of tropical rainforest. Copán was buried in deep tropical jungle until the forest was cut down to plant tobacco and corn at the end of the 19th century.

Even without its tropical greenery, Copán remains one of the loveliest ruins dating from the Classic period of the Maya (300–800 CE).

RECONSTRUCTING THE MAYA

Copán ranks among the most important Mayan sites because of the vast number of hieroglyphic texts that have been discovered there. Most of these are carved onto large stelae (inscribed stone slabs), altars and architectural stones. Mayan hieroglyphics represent a complete writing system, which is both pictorial and phonetic. There are more than 800 Mayan signs and each one stands for a word or syllable, which means that Mayan inscriptions can be read aloud more or less as they were written centuries ago. The gradual deciphering of these texts – a process that is still ongoing – has given experts a unique window into Mayan society and history.

For instance, one of the great treasures of Copán is the magnificent Hieroglyphic Stairway, which was constructed during the 8th century. Its 2,000-plus hieroglyphic inscriptions recount the history of Copán's

rulers, from the time of its founder, K'inich Yax K'uk' Mo (Great-Sun First Quetzal Macaw, fl. 426 CE), through its most famous ruler, Uaxaclajuun Ub'aah K'awiil (18-Rabbit, 695–738 CE). (All dates given for Mayan rulers refer to the approximate years they reigned.) During the reign of 18-Rabbit, who was the 13th ruler of Copán, the structure known as the Acropolis and most of the other important ceremonial monuments,

Right The Ball Court at Copán is the most imposing and decorative in Meso-America. The narrow playing alley was bordered by slanting benches topped with large carved stones, which were formerly covered with stucco.

including the Great Plaza and the Ball Court, took their final form.

Archeological exploration of Copán's monuments, though challenging, has also yielded important discoveries. Rather than destroying later structures to get at the earlier levels of construction, as previous archeologists had done, current excavations involve digging tunnels into Copán's huge Acropolis. In 1996–1997 an archeological team from the University of Pennsylvania dug such a tunnel and discovered a small temple platform deep inside the Acropolis. Inside this structure, they unearthed tombs that were found to contain the cinnabar-covered bones of a man who is believed to have been Copán's first ruler, K'inich Yax K'uk' Mo, and those of an elderly woman who may have been his widow. Both tombs were filled with lavish offerings, including jade carvings and ceramics.

Also unearthed as recently as 1991 is a temple that had been buried almost intact under later buildings. The stuccoed façade of this temple, called the Rosalila Structure, features carved images of Mayan gods and has given historians a good idea of the splendour of Mayan architecture when it was first constructed.

REDISCOVERY AND EXPLORATION

By the time of the Spanish conquest of Honduras in the 1520s, Copán had long been overgrown by rainforest. Historians believe that the first report of the existence of Copán was contained in a letter written by the Spanish emissary Don Diego Garcia De Palacios to King Philip II of Spain in 1576. However, Copán's site remained virtually unknown until it was visited by a series of explorers during the early 19th century. Juan Galindo, a Central American explorer and army officer of Spanish, English and Irish descent, wrote a description of the ruins in 1834. His account attracted the interest of American explorer and travel writer John Lloyd Stephens and his associate, British architect and artist Frederick Catherwood, who included the site in their influential illustrated book *Incidents of Travel in Yucatan* (1842).

Left The Hieroglyphic Stairway, completed in the 8th century, has 63 steps, each one embellished with glyphs. Deciphering this text of over 2,000 characters has helped researchers reconstruct the history of the Mayan dynasties.

WHY DID COPÁN COLLAPSE?

Unfortunately the deciphering of Copán's hieroglyphics does not explain the biggest mystery surrounding the Maya: why the great city-states of the lowland rainforest collapsed and were abandoned during the 9th century. Most archeologists of Mayan sites now agree that three factors contributed to the downfall: a dramatic increase in wars between the city-states; overpopulation leading to environmental collapse; and prolonged drought. When the population of the Mayan city-states increased beyond the agricultural capacity of the fragile soil of the rainforest, and Mayan priests were unable to call down the rains from their rain god Chaak, wars between cities over natural resources and food supplies – combined with the ravages of deforestation and erosion – brought to an end the most sophisticated pre-Columbian American culture.

Copán

A Classic-period ceremonial centre, such as the one at Copán, generally consisted of a series of stepped platforms topped with masonry structures, including towering temple-pyramids. The platforms were arranged around broad plazas or courtyards. The exterior façade of these structures was highly embellished with colourful painted stucco reliefs.

The buildings surrounding the plazas, often called palaces, were administrative centres. Seated on benches covered with jaguar skins, the city's ruler would receive tribute, make judicial rulings and entertain visitors. In the courtyards more public activities, such as sacred dances, blood-letting and prisoner sacrifices, took place.

This ceremonial centre was the hub of a sophisticated civilization with an advanced calendar, a complex written language and a comprehensive system of astronomy. At the city's height, at about 800 CE, some 20,000 people lived in Copán and its vicinity. Food for the urban residents was produced in rural settlements in the Copán River valley, a fertile bottom land that attracted early agriculturalists to the region more than 3,000 years ago. The collapse of Copán from causes such as overpopulation, environmental stress, political unrest and warfare is a common theme among many lost cities.

① ACROPOLIS

Copán's main structural grouping is the Acropolis. It overlooks the Copán River, which flows past the city's eastern border. Over time the Acropolis was added to and remodelled, with new structures built over old ones.

② HIEROGLYPHIC STAIRWAY

This grand staircase leading up to the Acropolis from the west was built in its current form by Copán's 13th ruler, Uaxaclajuun Ub'aah K'awiil (18-Rabbit), in the early 8th century. Its inscriptions record the birth, parentage, accession to power, important achievements and death of the most distinguished rulers of the city. Later, Copán's 15th ruler, K'ak' Yipyaj Chan K'awiil (Smoke Shell, 749–763), doubled the stairway's length, adding extra inscriptions and framing balustrades. By tunnelling into the Acropolis under the Hieroglyphic Stairway, archeologists also revealed an Early Classic temple, known as the Rosalila structure, built by Copán's tenth ruler, Moon Jaguar, around 571 CE. The temple is completely intact and covered with the most elaborately decorated façade yet discovered at Copán. Even part of the roof crest that originally topped many Mayan temples has been preserved. A replica of the Rosalila created from archeologists' drawings is the star exhibit at the Sculpture Museum at Copán, which opened in 1996.

③ POPUL NAH

On the west side of the Acropolis was the Popul Nah, or Council House. The structure is sometimes called the Great Mat House because enormous mats carved in mosaic stone decorated the building's upper surfaces. On the upper wall are portraits of Mayan lords seated on glyphs (decorative symbols) that some archeologists think might represent the locality they governed. Meetings were held under the sun and stars on the wide porch in front of the structure, rather than inside.

④ ALTAR Q

At the base of the stairway in the West Court of the Acropolis is a square monument of enormous archeological importance. Around the four sides of this box-shaped stone are carved portraits of the 16 rulers of Copán. Each is seated on a glyph of his name, which serves as a throne. The monument was dedicated by Copán's last ruler, Yax Pasaj Chan Yopaat (First Dawned Sky Lightening God, 763–c. 810).

⑤ BALL COURT

Copán's ball court, between the Acropolis and the Great Plaza, is the most perfect of any to be found at Classic-period Mayan sites. Sculptures in the shape of macaw heads served as markers, and the doorways, jambs and façades of the surrounding temples were ornamented with carved figures of the rain god Chaak and other deities. At its north end are at least 63 carved stelae and 14 altar structures. Spectators stood on stepped platforms to watch the ball game. How the game was played and its ritual meaning are not yet understood.

⑥ GREAT PLAZA

To the north of the Acropolis is the Great Plaza, built by 18-Rabbit and filled with monuments in his honour. Stelae depict him in the guise of various deities, such as wearing the jade-decorated costume of the maize god. Other monuments on the plaza link 18-Rabbit to the Mayan creation myth. The arrangement of monuments on the plaza may be linked to cosmic events, such as the movements of Venus and the constellations.

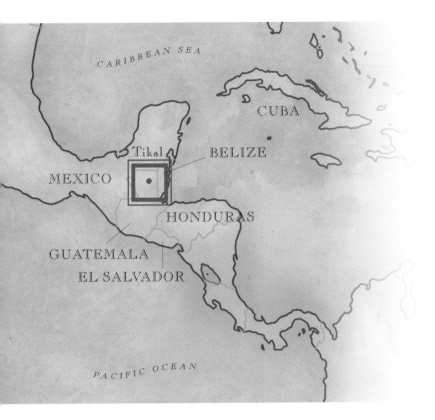

Tikal – Mayan metropolis

One of the largest Classic-period Mayan sites is Tikal, in the lowland rainforest of Guatemala. The ruins stretch for more than 15.5 square km (6 square miles) and contain about 3,000 structures, ranging from lofty temple-pyramids and huge palaces to individual household huts. Historians estimate that at its height, between 200 and 850 CE, from 45,000 to as many as 100,000 people lived in the city.

Like other Classic-period Mayan centres, the city declined in the 9th century due to wars, overpopulation and drought.

DYNASTIES AND INVASIONS

Tikal's history, as documented by inscription texts, supports the idea that warfare between city-states contributed to the collapse of the Mayan culture. Texts name Yax Ehb' Xook as the founder and first ruler of Tikal during the 1st century. Tikal's eighth ruler, Chak Tok Ich'aak (Great Jaguar Paw, *c.* 360–378), is recorded as having died on 14 January 378 – the very same day that a person named Sihyaj K'ahk' (Fire is Born) arrived in Tikal.

Historians believe that these two events are connected and that the 'arrival' of Fire is Born actually refers to the invasion of Tikal by warriors from the powerful military city of Teotihuacan (see pages 164–165) in central Mexico. The invaders probably executed Great Jaguar Paw and installed a new dynasty loyal to Teotihuacan as its rulers. A stone stela bears a carved portrait of Yax Nuun Ahiin, who was *ajaw* (king) of Tikal until 411 CE, dressed in the style of a Teotihuacan warrior. In his right hand he carries an *atlatl* (spear-thrower), and in his left a shield bearing the face of the Teotihuacan war god, Tlatoc.

In the last half of the 6th century another significant invasion altered the fortunes of Tikal. According to inscriptions, in 562 CE Tikal was attacked and conquered by warriors from the city-state of Caracol, formerly Tikal's ally. For the next 130 years no commemorative stelae were erected in the city, and archeologists have found evidence that public monuments were damaged on purpose.

MONUMENTAL TIKAL

In the first decades of the 7th century Tikal resumed its former glory. The heart of the city was a Great Plaza, with temple-pyramids to the east and west. North of the plaza was the Acropolis, and south was a palace complex. Groups of buildings were connected to the Great Plaza and to each other by causeways. Because water was scarce, Tikal had several large reservoirs surrounded by embankments, to provide water during the dry season.

The complex at Tikal boasts six impressive temple-pyramids, the tallest of which measures 70 metres (230 feet) high. The temple-pyramids were constructed from limestone blocks, which covered a rubble core. Small rooms inside the pyramids were entered only by priests and nobles during ceremonial occasions.

'Laid to rest with the king were his jade and shell ornaments, vessels filled with food and drink, and a collection of bones incised with scenes from Tikal's mythic and historical past.'

Several of the temple-pyramids are also tombs. Discovered beneath Temple I in 1962, for instance, was the splendid funerary shrine and tomb of Jasaw Chan K'awiil (682–734 CE). Laid to rest with the king were his jade and shell ornaments, vessels filled with food and drink, and a collection of bones that had been delicately incised with scenes from Tikal's mythic and historical past. On the temple's summit is a huge roof comb portraying the ruler seated on his throne.

Tikal has fewer important stelae or stone sculptures than other Classic-period Mayan sites. However, beautiful reliefs depicting the city's rulers with inscription texts are carved into the wooden lintels above the doorways of several of the temples.

EXPLORATION AND EXCAVATION

It is doubtful that Tikal was ever really lost, but the first Westerner to see it was probably Franciscan monk Antonio de Avendano in 1695. Several scientific expeditions visited Tikal to investigate, map and photograph the site in the late 19th and early 20th centuries, including British archeologist Alfred Maudslay, who published detailed drawings of its monuments after visiting the site in the 1890s. In 1951 a small airstrip was built so that archeologists could reach the ruins without several days of travel through the jungle on foot or by mule.

The most extensive work at Tikal has been carried out by the University Museum of the University of Pennsylvania. By 1970 its team working on the Tikal Project included more than 100 archeologists and specialists. In additional to clearing and restoring many of the structures in Tikal, in cooperation with the Guatemalan government, the project made numerous important discoveries and published detailed drawings of many of Tikal's monuments, to aid scholars in deciphering their inscriptions.

Left As at other Classic-period Mayan sites, the central acropolis at Tikal features a series of stepped platforms topped by pyramid temples and palaces (administrative centres), built around broad plazas.

Palenque – jewel of Mayan artistry

Palenque is considered by many to be the most beautiful Mayan city. Its setting is magical: it sits at the base of a chain of limestone hills covered with tall rainforest, just above the floodplain of the Usamacinta River, in what is now the Mexican state of Chiapas.

Palenque is smaller than the other great Mayan cities of Copán and Tikal. However, the site contains some of the finest architecture, sculpture and carvings that the Maya created.

TEMPLES AND TOMBS

At its height in the 7th century, Palenque was a densely populated city with more than 1,000 structures. Facing a plaza on the eastern side of Palenque is what many consider the most aesthetically pleasing Mayan building still surviving, the Temple of the Sun. The temple is very well preserved (including its elaborate roof comb and relief carvings) and sits on a stepped platform with a steep central stairway. Inside, in an inner vaulted chamber, is a miniature version of the larger temple, containing a magnificent carved tablet with an image of the jaguar god of the Underworld. The Temple of the Sun and two similar temples were built by the successor and son of Palenque's greatest king, K'inich Janahb' Pakal (Pacal the Great, 615–683 CE).

Pacal the Great ruled over Palenque from the time he was 12 until his death at the age of 80. He was also responsible for the construction of Palenque's other most famous building, the Temple of Inscriptions. It, too, sits at the top of a stepped pyramid with a grand front stairway. More than 620 hieroglyphs, including many dates, are carved into three of its interior walls.

In June 1952, the Mexican archeologist Alberto Ruz discovered a rubble-filled stairway underneath one of the large stone slabs flooring the Temple of Inscriptions. It took several years of work to clear the stairway, which descends 24 metres (80 feet) below the floor of the upper temple. After removing another slab blocking the subterranean entrance, Ruz gazed into the tomb of Pacal the Great himself (as was established by deciphering the inscriptions).

Right *Built in the late 7th century, Palenque's Temple of the Sun stands on a stepped platform with a frontal stairway. The temple's four-sided, sloping roof is topped by an elaborate comb.*

Left *Nestled in the lush tropical rainforest of present-day Chiapas, Mexico, are the Palace and Tower of the city of Palenque. To the left is the towering Temple of Inscriptions, with its grand front staircase.*

PALENQUE AND MAYAN COSMOLOGY

The artistry and decorations of Palenque's monuments reflect Mayan cosmological beliefs. For them, the starry heavens, this world and the Underworld were linked by a World Tree. Dead souls travelled along the Tree as they descended into the Underworld or rose into the heavens. Though Pacal the Great is shown falling into the centipede-like jaws of the Underworld in the carving on his sarcophagus lid, the mask of the maize god in which he was entombed indicates that, like the maize, he will rise again and ascend the World Tree to paradise.

Another cosmological tale is told by the Sun Temple and its two sister temples. Each is dedicated to a different deity in the Mayan pantheon and tells a different part of the Mayan creation myth. The Temple of the Cross links scenes from the creation myth to Pacal the Great and other kings of the Palenque dynasty, all of which are carved around an image of the World Tree. The Temple of the Foliated Cross honours the origins of agricultural bounty, with carvings of the Tree of Maize and the Mountain of Sustenance. The Temple of the Sun, with its carving of the jaguar god, is dedicated to the birth of war.

The great king's sarcophagus is covered with an intricately carved slab that shows him falling into the Underworld. Among the treasures buried with the king is an exquisite lifesize jade mask of the maize god, with eyes fashioned of jade and obsidian. It seems that Pacal the Great, like the Egyptian pharaohs, had built during his lifetime his own lavish funerary monument.

CURRENT EXPLORATIONS

Discoveries are still being made at the site of Palenque. In 1999 Alfonso Morales, the chief archeologist of the Palenque Cross Group Project, discovered a 1,500-year-old bench or throne covered with carvings and inscriptions. A similar bench or throne was unearthed in 2002 by archeologists belonging to Mexico's National Institute of Anthropology and History.

The reliefs on the 2002 find are extraordinary. In the centre is Palenque's great king, Pacal the Great, reborn as a legendary ruler from 252 BCE. He is passing down the lineage of kingship to future rulers, including his grandson and great-grandson. This great-grandson, K'inich Ahkal Mo' Nahb, who ruled Palenque in the early 8th century, constructed the temples where the benches were found.

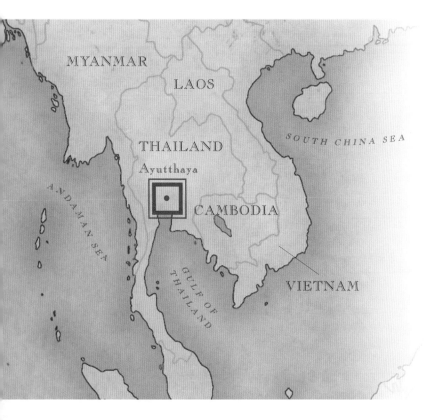

Ayutthaya – ancient Thai capital

Ayutthaya was the capital of the ancient Thai kingdom that became the nation of Siam – today, modern Thailand. Founded in 1350 CE, the city sits on a tropical island at the confluence of three rivers, 80 km (50 miles) north of Bangkok. In the early 17th century, Ayutthaya experienced a golden age in which art and culture flourished.

During this time, the city had close ties to foreign powers, including the court of Louis XIV of France. However, in 1767 a power closer to home besieged and largely destroyed Ayutthaya, eclipsing its glory.

GOLDEN CITY OF RAMA

U Thong, the leader of the kingdom of Ayutthaya in the 14th century, founded the city of Ayutthaya as his new capital. He named it after Ayodhya in northern India, city of the hero Rama in the Hindu epic the Ramayana (in Sanskrit, the name means 'unassailable'). Styling himself as a new Rama, U Thong took the royal name of King Ramathibodi (reigned 1350–1369), declared Theravada Buddhism as Ayutthaya's official religion and built many Buddhist temples near his capital city. One of them, Wat Yai Chai Mongkol, built in 1357 as a meditation site for monks returning from pilgrimages to Sri Lanka, is famous for its huge statue of a reclining Buddha (a *wat* is a collection of religious buildings surrounded by a wall with gateways). The wat's large *chedi* (dome-shaped tower), which was built in 1592 to commemorate a military victory and was

relatively undamaged when the city fell, dominates the skyline of the old city.

Many of the important monuments in Ayutthaya were constructed during the 15th century. In 1424, for example, King Boromaraja II (reigned 1424–1448) built the temple complex of Wat Ratburana, to hold the ashes of his elder brothers, who killed each other in a battle on elephant-back. They were fighting over which one of them would be king. The wat's tall *prang* (geometrical tower) is decorated with stucco statues of mythical animals. In 1957 archeologists discovered a sealed vault beneath the temple filled with golden jewellery and Buddha statues.

In 1448 King Boromtrailokanat (reigned 1448–1488) built Wat Phra Si Sanphet, a grand temple in the centre of the ancient capital. The temple housed a glorious standing Buddha statue, 16 metres (53 feet) tall, originally covered by more than 150 kg (330 lb) of gold. The wat also featured three large, bell-shaped chedis, which were built to contain the ashes of King Boromtrailokanat and his two sons, one of whom succeeded his father. When it was constructed, the wat's

main temple was connected directly to the royal palace.

By the end of the 16th century Ayutthaya was the strongest military and commercial power in South-East Asia. The city had trade and diplomatic ties with Portugal, Japan, Holland, Denmark, England and France. Foreign traders were made welcome in Ayutthaya, and some were permitted to set up small villages outside the city walls. Ayutthaya's cosmopolitan attitude was largely due to King Narai (reigned 1656–1688), who permitted the Dutch and English trading companies to establish factories in Ayutthaya, sent diplomatic missions to Paris and The Hague and invited French engineers to construct fortifications and build a new royal palace.

AYUTTHAYA'S FALL AND RECONSTRUCTION

But Ayutthaya's foreign friends could not help it survive against enemies closer to home. Over its 400-year history, Ayutthaya had many conflicts with Burma. In 1569 Burmese forces managed to capture the city and carried off the royal family. Ayutthaya's

independence was restored by King Naresuan (reigned 1590–1605), the son of the vassal king installed by the Burmese.

After a period of peace in the second quarter of the 18th century, when art, literature and learning flourished, Burma again invaded Ayutthaya, this time with devastating results. Following a lengthy siege, the city surrendered and was sacked and burned in 1767. Its art treasures, libraries and monuments were almost totally destroyed. Ayutthaya became a ghost town,

its people dead or displaced. Only the chedi and prang towers continued to stand above the temple ruins.

Over the last 150 years many of Ayutthaya's historical structures have been reconstructed. The ruins have also been extensively studied by archeologists and art historians. Recently the University of Melbourne, working in conjunction with Chulalongkorn University in Bangkok, has developed a virtual-reality reconstruction of Ayutthaya at its height, c. 1600.

Above *The three bell-shaped chedis of Wat Phra Si Sanphet were built in 1448 to hold the ashes of King Boromtrailokanat and his two sons, one of whom reigned as King Boromtrailokanat II.*

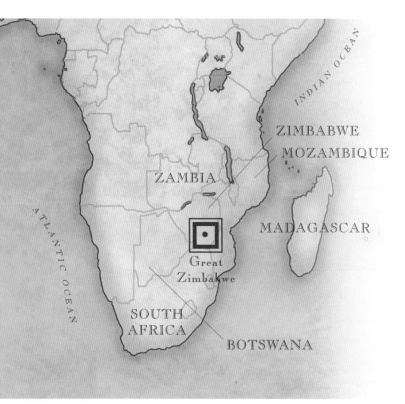

Great Zimbabwe – trading city

The largest ruins complex in Africa, Great Zimbabwe sits on a wooded plain surrounded by hills in today's Zimbabwe. Settled around 350 CE by the Shona people, Great Zimbabwe was the capital of a major trading kingdom known as the Munhumutapa Empire. European and Arab traders first came to the city in search of the biblical town of Ophir, from which the Queen of Sheba supplied gold for the Temple of Solomon.

Although they did not find Ophir, traders did discover an indigenous African city with which they could trade for gold, ivory and cattle.

RUINS AND MYSTERIES

The vast ruins of Great Zimbabwe present many mysteries. Built from 1100 to 1450 CE, the city was once home to an estimated 12,000–20,000 people. Its many structures and interlocking walls were built entirely of stone, employing a dry-stone technique in which no mortar is used to bind the stone blocks. The granite blocks were cut and laid in courses so skilfully that the walls are still standing after seven centuries.

The ruins can be divided into two distinct architectural groups. The Hill Complex includes what some historians believe was a ritual enclosure, a smelting enclosure and an iron-keeping enclosure, though the actual uses for the spaces cannot be absolutely determined. The Valley Complex includes Great Zimbabwe's most impressive ruin, the Great Enclosure. Its main feature is a massive but graceful curved granite wall, 1.2 metres (4 feet) thick, as much as 9.75 metres (32 feet) high and 244 metres (800 feet) long. Inside, other walls subdivide the enclosure into narrow passageways, platforms and what may be individual rooms or dwellings. The most mysterious feature of the Great Enclosure is a large conical tower that stands 9 metres (30 feet) high. It is completely solid, without doors, windows or stairs, and offers no clues as to its use.

Archeological artefacts, such as shards of Chinese pottery, coins from Arabia and glass beads from non-local sources, suggest that Great Zimbabwe functioned as a centre for trading. Radiocarbon dating of these finds dates the oldest to the 1200s. Evidence also suggests that, in addition to gold and ivory, metals such as iron, tin and copper were traded to European and Arab merchants, as well as cattle and cowrie shells.

The final mystery surrounding Great Zimbabwe is why it declined and was abandoned around 1450 CE. Explanations include overpopulation, depleted land resources due to over-farming and drought – reasons very similar to those proposed to explain the collapse of the great Mayan cities half a world away.

POLITICS AND CONTROVERSY

Ever since the first modern Europeans visited Great Zimbabwe, the site has been the focus of controversy. Unwilling to believe that sub-Saharan Africans could have built a

'European and Arab traders first came to the city in search of the biblical town of Ophir, from which the Queen of Sheba had supplied gold for the Temple of Solomon.'

Right Inside the Great Enclosure stands a mysterious conical tower. Constructed of dry-stone blocks and without doors, windows or stairs, its purpose and uses are unknown.

sophisticated city, 19th- and early 20th-century theorists, who were motivated more by politics than by the evidence, proposed that Portuguese travellers, Arabs, Chinese, Persians – even the lost tribes of Israel – were the builders of Great Zimbabwe. The first modern European to visit the site, German geologist Carl Mauch in 1871, stated that it must have been built by a 'civilized nation' and resurrected the medieval idea that the Hill Complex was a copy of the Temple of Solomon and that the Great Enclosure must have been built by the Queen of Sheba.

ARCHEOLOGY AND RECENT FINDS

In 1905 British archeologist David Randall-MacIver studied the remains of the mud structures sited within the Great Enclosure and concluded that the ruins were 'unquestionably African in every detail'.

Later scientific investigations have shown that the walls of the Great Enclosure once surrounded houses built of *daga*, a gravel conglomerate, stained a robust red colour. Although few traces of the houses remain today, the superb construction of the city's granite walls gives an indication of the capital's former greatness. Some experts have theorized that the Great Enclosure may have been a royal residence; others that the city might also have been a religious centre, as suggested by stone monoliths and altar-like structures.

The most intriguing find has been the birds carved from soapstone that have been discovered throughout the site. The ruins of Great Zimbabwe have become the sacred shrine of modern Zimbabwe, and the soapstone bird is the country's national symbol, depicted on its flag.

Below No one knows the function of the Great Enclosure. While some researchers speculate that the walls enclosed a royal residence, others believe that it may have had sacred or ritual uses.

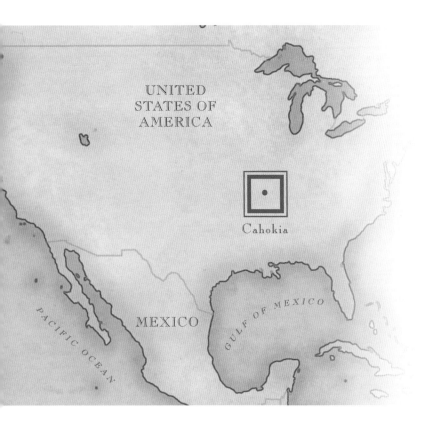

Cahokia – woodland mounds

The largest city north of Meso-America before the arrival of Columbus was Cahokia, a Native American settlement located at the confluence of the Missouri, Illinois and Mississippi Rivers, near what is now Collinsville in Illinois. The city's archeological legacy comprises more than 120 earthen mounds, among which is the largest ancient earthwork in the Americas.

The mounds – really flat-topped pyramids – were places of burial and ceremony, as well as pedestals atop which the leaders of Cahokia lived and ruled.

NATIVE AMERICAN METROPOLIS
Cahokia was settled in about 700 CE by a Native American people whose name is now lost. The French missionary monks who rediscovered the site in the mid-1700s named it 'Cahokia' after a tribal group that did not reach the area until the 1600s. The early settlers were probably nomadic hunter gatherers who found the rich soil of the Mississippi River valley ideal for cultivating corn and other starchy seed crops. With a reliable source of food, the population increased and the villages grew into cities.

At its height, Cahokia was a complex hierarchical society, in which an elite class controlled a population of trades-workers, artisans and farmers. As many as 40,000 people may have lived at Cahokia. Hoes with flint blades, axes with shaped stone heads, pottery and ornaments made of shell beads were traded with other river-side settlements in return for copper, salt and minerals.

The largest earthwork at Cahokia, which the monks who rediscovered the city named Monk's Mound, stands about 30.5 metres (100 feet) high, with a base 316 metres (1,037 feet) long and 240 metres (790 feet) wide. Its construction in around 1000 CE required workers to haul more than 14 million baskets of dirt. Excavations have revealed that a large building, perhaps the residence of the chief, was sited on the top of the mound. South of Monk's Mound is a flat, open plaza, which shows evidence of having been skilfully levelled. A wooden stockade with guard towers surrounded the city.

Excavation of another mound, Mound 72, has given archeologists insights into the city's culture. Under the mound are the remains of a man buried around 1050 CE. Probably an important leader, he was laid to rest on a bed of 20,000 shell disc beads arranged in the shape of a falcon. Near by are 800 unused arrows with finely made heads.

Buried with him were four men with their heads and hands cut off, and 53 young women who had been strangled. Evidence suggests that these were human sacrifices.

Another recent find is the remains of a ring of cedar posts that functioned as a solar calendar. When aligned with a key post outside the circle, the equinoctial sun appears to rise directly out of Monk's Mound. Other positions in the ring were calibrated to the solstices.

'This was a complex hierarchical society, in which an elite class controlled trades-workers, artisans and farmers.'

WHY DID CAHOKIA DECLINE?

The decline of Cahokia between 1250 and 1400 CE exemplifies the demise of many ancient cities. As the population of Cahokia grew, over-farming and unchecked erosion caused by tree-cutting on nearby bluffs reduced the amount of arable land. As a result, the surrounding farms could no longer produce sufficient food.

Tree-cutting was a particular problem at Cahokia. Historians estimate that the city's stockade fence would have required as many as 20,000 tree poles. Tree-cutting made it more difficult for people to collect firewood, and it also destroyed the habitat of wild game that could be hunted for meat. Moreover, when the trees were cleared, erosion caused water levels to increase, making some farmland marshy and useless.

Environmental changes and disease probably also played a part in Cahokia's end. A global cooling trend in about 1250 CE may have shortened the growing season. As the city's population increased, so did the likelihood of epidemics of dysentery and tuberculosis, since the city had no sanitary system for disposing of garbage and waste.

When life at Cahokia grew difficult, people may have left to follow herds of migrating buffalo. As the population declined, the city may also have come under attack from nearby settlements. As a result of all these factors, by 1400 Cahokia was largely deserted.

Left *The most famous of Cahokia's mounds is Monk's Mound, the largest such mound in the Americas. Its flat top shows evidence that a chief's house or religious structure once stood there.*

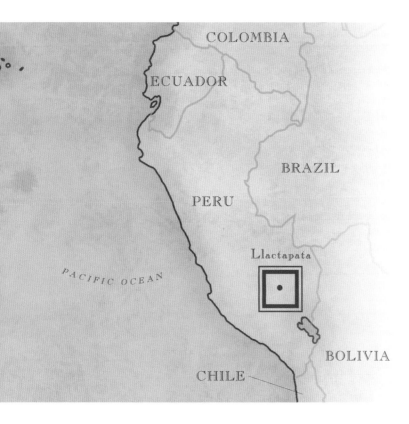

Llactapata – observatory of the Incas

In 2003, a team of British and American explorers located Llactapata, an Incan settlement within 5 km (3 miles) of Machu Picchu, Peru. Though the explorers knew of Llactapata from the field notes of Hiram Bingham, who rediscovered Machu Picchu, the ruins were so well hidden that explorers had to hack their way through the jungle with machetes to examine the site.

Incorporating more than 80 structures, Llactapata is particularly interesting to archeologists because many of its ruins are aligned astronomically with structures in nearby Machu Picchu.

ASTRONOMICAL OBSERVATORY

The site, on a long ridge facing Machu Picchu and the two mountain peaks on either side of it, looks towards Machu Picchu over the Aobamba canyon, whose river carries glacial meltwater down from the Andean heights. When Bingham visited Llactapata he seems to have been more interested in its wonderful view looking towards Machu Picchu than he was in the site's unique features.

Recent explorations have focused on clearing and studying the Llactapata ruins and investigating their purpose. In addition to several large, well-constructed stone buildings and two courtyards, investigators have discovered two ceremonial corridors, which they surmise functioned as a sun temple. The longer corridor, measuring 33 metres (108 feet), has no side doors or side passages. However, its length frames a window along the horizon that is aligned to the rising of the Pleiades star cluster, an event that precedes sunrise by about 15 minutes at the time of the June solstice.

There is additional evidence to suggest that Llactapata served as an astronomical observatory. U-shaped structures with niches attached to outside walls of the ceremonial corridors are also aligned to the June-solstice sunrise and the Pleiades. A solitary structure called the Overlook Temple seems to have been both a June-solstice and an equinox feature, placed so as to view the sunrise over the tops of Cerro San Miguel and Machu Picchu mountains on these significant days. Investigators theorize that the Inca ruler and his retinue may have followed an Incan processional road from Machu Picchu to Llactapata on special occasions to celebrate the rising of the sun.

Experts studying the site are also looking for evidence that Llactapata is one of a number of natural and constructed features surrounding Machu Picchu that may together have functioned as an elaborate geographical 'calendar'. These significant features include sight lines to sacred mountains, springs, unusual rocks, caves, carved rocks, fountains and pools. Such features may have transformed the whole neighbourhood of Machu Picchu, including the site of Llactapata, into a sacred landscape with astronomical, cosmological and spiritual significance.

REDISCOVERY AND EXCAVATION

The leaders of the team studying Llactapata, Briton Hugh Thompson and American Gary Ziegler, tried using high-tech methods to map the location of Llactapata's ruins. In May 2003 two flights were made over the area to collect thermal infrared remote-sensing images. However, the jungle vegetation covering the ruins was so dense that the technique proved only partially successful. Like many Andes explorers before them, the team ultimately had to rely on mules to climb up to the ridge at 2,760 metres (9,050 feet) and to use machetes to clear a path to the site.

In addition to the astronomical links to Machu Picchu, investigations have revealed that Llactapata may have been an important staging post on a network of roads that

connected Cusco to the ruined Incan cities of Vitcos and Vilcabamba. The site may also have been a resting place and roadside shrine for official parties on their way to Machu Picchu. Excavations have uncovered a number of simple foundations, indicating that Llactapata may have been home to as many as 300 permanent residents, many of whom worked in support of activities at Machu Picchu. For example, crops grown at Llactapata may have supplemented Machu Picchu's food supplies in season, when large parties were in residence.

After Spanish conquistadors captured and executed the last Inca leader, Tupac Amaru, in 1572, the Incas deserted their cities and towns. Though some of these lost Incan cities have been rediscovered, many more may still be hiding under dense jungle foliage, waiting to reveal their secrets.

Above From Llactapacta, the site of Machu Picchu is visible across the Aobamba canyon. Many of Llactapacta's buildings are aligned astronomically with those at Machu Picchu.

'On special occasions, the Inca ruler and his retinue may have followed an Incan processional road from Machu Picchu to Llactapata to celebrate the rising of the sun.'

Ciudad Blanca – legend of the Mosquito Coast

Legends persist of a fabulous pre-Columbian city known as Ciudad Blanca, or White City, hidden in the dense jungles of the Mosquito Coast of Honduras. The first European to search for Ciudad Blanca was Spanish conquistador Hernán Cortés, who failed in his attempts to locate the city. Since that time Ciudad Blanca has attracted many adventurers and treasure-seekers.

Attempts to locate the ruins using satellite-based remote-sensing technology have recently made significant finds. Perhaps in the next few years expeditions will locate the capital of an undocumented civilization that is an important link between the indigenous cultures of North and South America.

LEGENDS OF THE WHITE CITY

The Pech people, an indigenous group that may have settled in Honduras during a migration from South to North America 7,000 years ago, are the source of the original legends about Ciudad Blanca. According to Pech oral history, the city was called Patatahua. It was constructed by Pech spirits or gods and was inhabited by the ancestors of present-day Pech. Stories say that the city was built of large white stones and featured carved images of animals, including lions and monkeys.

Other ancient sources say Ciudad Blanca was the place of origin of Quetzalcóatl (Feathered Serpent), the culture hero of the Mayan, Toltec, Aztec and other Meso-American civilizations. In some versions of the myth, Quetzalcóatl was descended from

a race of white-skinned people (or he wore a white mask). By the time the Spanish arrived in Honduras in the early 16th century, stories say, the famed city was in decline or already abandoned.

In 1526, less than five years after conquering Tenochtitlan (see pages 60–63), Cortés unsuccessfully searched the north coast of Honduras for a city he believed had wealth to rival the riches of the Aztec empire. In 1544 Christobal de Pedraza, Bishop of Honduras, wrote a letter to the King of Spain describing the ruins of a large city he had

seen when looking east from a mountaintop into one of the river valleys of the Mosquito Coast. His native guides, he wrote, told him that the nobles who had lived in the city ate from golden plates.

EXPEDITIONS AND DISCOVERIES

The most famous modern expedition to search for Ciudad Blanca took place in 1939, sponsored by the American Indian Museum of the Heye Foundation of New York. Led by American explorer Theodore Morde, the expedition spent five months cutting

Left Quetzalcóatl is the mythic deity and culture hero from whom almost all Meso-American people claim descent. He was central to Meso-American art and religion for almost 2,000 years, from the pre-Classic era until the Spanish conquest.

through dense vegetation and navigating miles of uncharted waterways in dugout canoes. On his return, Morde claimed to have found the walled ruins of the lost city along a river bordered by pure white sand. The ruins covered a large area and contained the remains of several big buildings, suggesting that the city once had a population of thousands.

These ruins, Morde said, also contained the remains of a temple dedicated to a monkey god, with a paved stairway marked by large stone columns decorated with carved monkeys and banisters with the carved images of a spider and a crocodile. Though Morde declined to reveal the exact location of the ruins, he published an account of his finds called *The City of the Monkey God*. While in London seeking funds for a return trip to Honduras, Morde was struck and killed by a car, an event that some believe was not an accident, but rather an attempt by people connected with him to keep the location of Ciudad Blanca secret. According to this speculation, these people knew that Morde would have to reveal the city's location to secure expedition funds and wanted to claim Ciudad Blanca's riches for themselves.

Several expeditions are now looking for Ciudad Blanca. The most ambitious, in 1997–1998, was sponsored by the Society for the Exploration and Preservation of the History of the Americas. Using remote-sensing images taken by Japanese and European satellites, the expedition tried to pinpoint the location of the ruins – a difficult task, since even radar cannot fully penetrate the vegetation of a tropical forest. Newly developed image-enhancement techniques revealed three possible sites, including one with what may be the ruins of a large ceremonial centre. Archeological teams from Honduras, the United States and Japan are currently planning expeditions to investigate these finds.

According to native legends, Ciudad Blanca may be not so much lost as hidden by the gods. Time will tell whether high-tech archeology will succeed in solving the intriguing mystery of this fabled lost city.

Left The dense jungle of the Mosquito Coast of Honduras is home to more than 275 species of birds, as well as to jaguars, ocelots and several species of monkeys. The foliage may also hide the ruins of the fabled lost city of Ciudad Blanca.

'According to native legends, Ciudad Blanca may be not so much lost as hidden by the gods.'

CHAPTER 5

CITIES OF KINGS, QUEENS AND EMPERORS

The cities in this section were the capitals and strongholds of ancient kings. In the Middle East, many of the kings date to biblical times. The temple tower built by Hammurabi, King of Babylon, may have inspired the story of the Tower of Babel in Genesis. Ramesses II, who may have been the Pharaoh of Exodus, contributed to the construction of the temple and tomb complex at Karnak. And the campaign of Nineveh's King Sennacherib against Jerusalem is recorded in 2 Kings.

Across the Mediterranean, these kings were giants of myth and history. The fall of Priam and the walled city of Troy is celebrated in Homer's *Iliad*. The greatest commander of the ancient world, Alexander the Great, died at Persepolis, which he had conquered. In the steppes of Asia, Genghis Khan and his son held court at their ceremonial capital at Karakorum. And in the Americas, the Toltec king Topiltzin, founder of Tula, called himself Quetzalcóatl to link his rule to the Feathered Serpent of Meso-American myth.

Cities of the great and the good

The stories of great ancient kings and queens often blur the line between mythology and history. The accounts of kings who are mentioned in the Bible, or in Greek and Roman epics and histories, have captured the popular imagination to such an extent that the rediscovery and excavation of their cities and citadels has sometimes focused on proving or disproving the historical accuracy of familiar stories.

In some cases this focus has been beneficial, as in the rediscovery of the site of Troy. In other cases the interpretation of archeological evidence has been unfairly influenced by the great stories of the past, as in the questionable reconstruction of the 'palace of King Minos' at Knossos in Crete.

KINGS OF THE BIBLE

The search for supporting evidence to prove the historical accuracy of the stories of biblical kings has been a strong theme in the exploration of the ancient cities of the Middle East. In the opinion of most modern scholars, the Bible is not an entirely reliable historical document. The corroborating archeological evidence has in some cases validated the stories of the Bible, but in others the evidence remains inconclusive.

Thebes, the ancient Egyptian city of temples and royal tombs, is a case in point. Though the dates now ascribed to Ramesses II, one of the principal builders of Thebes, do not match those when Moses was supposed to be in Egypt, Ramesses II is traditionally believed to have been the Pharaoh of the book of Exodus, who enslaved and then reluctantly freed the ancient Israelites.

On the other hand, a stela erected by Ramesses II in the late 13th century BCE mentions two conquered peoples who came to 'make obeisance to him'. Were the Israelites one of these peoples? The biblical account also states that while they were slaves in Egypt, the Israelites built for Pharaoh the supply cities of Pithom and Ra'amses. Ra'amses has been identified as Pi-Ramesse Aa-nakhtu, an ancient city in the Nile Delta enlarged by Ramesses II and used as a northern capital and military base for campaigns into the Levant and Canaan. If this identification is correct, it strengthens the case for Ramesses II being the Pharaoh of the Bible.

The ancient Assyrian city of Nineveh, now in modern Iraq, also has rich biblical associations. It was the stronghold of a series of powerful Assyrian kings, including Sennacherib, who conquered 46 cities in Judah, captured or deported more than 200,000 Judaeans and laid siege to Jerusalem itself. Two verses in 2 Kings tell the story: an angel defends the City of David by visiting the camp of the Assyrians in the night and killing 'an hundred fourscore and five thousand' (185,000) Assyrian soldiers in

Right *A relief of Sennacherib, King of Assyria from 704 to 681 BCE. The biblical account of his unsuccessful siege of Jerusalem differs from an inscription found during the excavation of his capital, Nineveh.*

their sleep. His army destroyed, Sennacherib returns in disgrace to Nineveh, where he is soon murdered by own sons.

Biblical scholars were very excited when excavation of Sennacherib's palace at Nineveh uncovered a cuneiform inscription giving the Assyrian king's own account of the siege of Jerusalem in 701 BCE. In Sennacherib's version, the siege was a mighty display of Assyrian power, during which the Assyrians constructed towers around the city to hem it in and raised banks of earth against its gates to prevent escape, shutting up the Judaean king Hezekiah 'like a bird in a cage'. Though he does not claim to have captured the city, Sennacherib does boast that he returned to Nineveh with a rich ransom of gold, silver and treasure from the besieged city.

Another ancient city that has strong biblical connections is Babylon, which is also found in modern-day Iraq. Hammurabi, Babylon's first great king, constructed a ziggurat or temple tower that may have inspired the Tower of Babel in the book of Genesis. In the Old Testament story, God objects to the presumptuous intent of the builders of the tower to 'reach unto Heaven'. To confound this effort, God causes a 'confusion of tongues' so that the builders cannot understand each other and scatters the people of Babylon over the face of the Earth. In Hebrew, the city's name comes from the verb *balal*, which means 'to confuse'. Biblical scholars explain that the identification of Babylon's ziggurat with the Tower of Babel probably stems from the fact that the book of Genesis took shape during the Babylonian captivity of the Hebrews, beginning in 597 BCE.

Right *This Colossus of Ramesses II stands at the Temple of Amun at Karnak. Ramesses II is usually identified as the Pharaoh of the biblical Exodus, who enslaved and then freed the ancient Israelites.*

RULERS OF GREEK AND ROMAN MYTH

Greek and Roman mythology has also spurred and shaped recent archeological exploration. The site identified as Troy in modern-day Anatolia, Turkey, has been the focus of mythology-inspired exploration since its rediscovery and initial excavation by German archeology enthusiast Heinrich Schliemann in the 1870s. It is likely that the site of Troy would never have been rediscovered, had Schliemann not been motivated to search for it by Homer's epics. However, his over-eager search for evidence of Homer's Troy led him to make some serious blunders, destroying evidence of other levels of habitation at Troy and leading to the early misidentification of artefacts found in the ruins.

In the *Iliad*, Paris has abducted Helen – the most beautiful woman in the world – the wife of King Menelaus of Sparta. To win her back (and perhaps gain control of Troy's sea-trade routes) the Greeks assemble an armada of 1,000 ships to lay siege to the city, led by Agamemnon of Mycenae, high king and brother of Menelaus. Famous warriors fight on each side, aided by the gods who favour them. When the Greek champion Achilles kills Hector, King Priam bravely enters the Greek camp at night to plead for the return of his son's body for a proper hero's funeral. In the end the Greeks are victorious. King Priam is killed by a son of Achilles, and Troy is sacked and burned.

The excavation of Knossos, the Bronze Age palace complex near Heraklion on the Greek island of Crete, has also been complicated by mythological speculations. When British amateur archeologist Sir Arthur Evans purchased and then excavated the site, he named the civilization he

discovered 'Minoan' after the famed King Minos of Greek mythology.

In Greek myth, Minos offends the sea god Poseidon by refusing to sacrifice a white bull sent by the god. To revenge this slight, Poseidon makes Minos' queen, Pasiphaë, fall in love with the bull. The offspring of their union is the monstrous Minotaur, who is imprisoned in a labyrinth constructed by the famed Athenian craftsman Daedalus, then living in exile at Knossos. The Athenian warrior Theseus, sent by Athens as tribute to King Minos, seduces Ariadne (Minos' daughter) into revealing the secret of the labyrinth. After killing the Minotaur, Theseus escapes from Knossos bearing Ariadne away with him and then abandons her on the Aegean island of Naxos.

This tale, which is celebrated in paintings, operas and novels, inspired and influenced Evans' archeological work. He interpreted and partially reconstructed the complex layout of the ruins he was excavating as 'labyrinthine' – so much so that the plan of the original building cannot now be determined. However, Evans' work did preserve many of the features of the site that might otherwise have been lost. The great staircase of the palace complex, for example, would have collapsed had Evans not restored it. Moreover, his important work laid the foundations on which contemporary study of Minoan society rests.

OTHER WELL-KNOWN EXAMPLES

Many of the other ancient royal cities described in this chapter have biblical, mythological or literary connections:

• Myths about the great Mayan culture hero Quetzalcóatl have mingled with the history of the great Toltec city of Tula and its founding king Topiltzin, who took the name Quetzalcóatl as a title of office when he assumed the kingship of the Toltecs.

• Virgil's *Aeneid* tells the story of the tragic ending of the love affair between Aeneas, son of King Priam of Troy, and Dido, Queen of Carthage. Carthage was the powerful city on the coast of North Africa that challenged the Roman Empire for control of the Mediterranean in the 2nd and 3rd centuries BCE.

• Nebuchadnezzar II, who ruled Babylon 1,000 years after Hammurabi, is an important character in the Old Testament. In the book of Daniel, Daniel interprets a prophetic dream for Nebuchadnezzar, and the Babylonian king also figures in events recorded in the biblical books of Ezekiel and 2 Kings.

• A detailed account of the destruction by fire of Persepolis, the great city founded by Darius the Great (now in modern Iran), appears in the works of the Greek historian Diodorus Siculus (*c.* 90–30 BCE). According to Diodorus, after the city was conquered by Alexander the Great, the palace of Xerxes was burned to the ground during a drunken revel, when a woman named Thais convinced Alexander to torch the city.

MACEDONIA

BULGARIA

BLACK SEA

AEGEAN SEA

Troy

TURKEY

MEDITERRANEAN SEA

Troy – city of the *Iliad*

Perhaps the most famous war saga of the ancient world is Homer's Iliad, *which tells the story of the siege and sack of the royal city of Troy (also called Ilium) in about 1190 BCE. Historians and archeologists have been searching for – and arguing about – the location of Troy for hundreds of years.*

Now, new excavations on the site in north-west Turkey that has been identified with Troy since the 19th century are revealing fresh information about this celebrated lost city.

HOMER'S TROY

In Homer's account, Troy was a well-walled, broad city with lofty gates and fine towers. Textual scholars point out that descriptions like these were standard conventions in epics of the time and could apply to many cities in addition to Troy. In the *Iliad* the palace of Troy's King Priam, his queen Hecuba and their famous offspring Hector, Paris and Cassandra was located within the walled citadel or upper town, which also had an *agora* (public marketplace) and probably sanctuaries or temples to Greek gods including Zeus, Apollo and Athena.

The positive identification of the site of the historical city of Troy is complicated by the fact that the actual events of the Trojan War preceded the composition of the *Iliad* by about 450 years. Although Homer was writing at the end of the 8th century BCE, the tale he told was probably part of an oral tradition of sung and recited epic poetry that reached back hundreds of years and would have combined elements of history and myth. Some archeologists doubt that the accuracy of Homer's account will ever be proved conclusively using archeological evidence, believing that the 'truth' of Homer's version of events is psychological and literary, rather than historical. Others argue that the general shape of the city as Homer described it might still have been recognizable from the remains at the time the *Iliad* was written.

DISCOVERY, EXCAVATIONS AND CONTROVERSY

Among those who believed absolutely in the historical accuracy of the *Iliad* was Heinrich Schliemann, a wealthy German businessman and archeology enthusiast. In the 1870s, he began excavations on a hill in north-west Anatolia, located 6 km (3½ miles) from the Dardanelles Strait.

Schliemann's methods were controversial, to say the least. Convinced that Homer's Troy lay at the deepest level of the hill, he dug a trench 40 metres (130 feet) wide straight through the hill. In his haste he dug right through the Homeric levels of Troy that he was seeking and destroyed many important structures. Nevertheless, in 1873 Schliemann announced that he had discovered Troy and unearthed a fabulous trove of gold and ornaments, which he called the 'Treasure of Priam'. Although later analysis proved that these finds date to 1,000 years before the supposed time of the Trojan War, Schliemann's identification of the site as Troy has held up, in the opinion of most archeologists.

What Schliemann did not immediately recognize is that Troy is actually best seen as a complex layer cake of cities that have been built one on top of another. Archeologists have identified nine levels of habitation at Troy, dating from the early Bronze Age (3000 BCE) up to the Byzantine era (about 1000 CE). Current thinking is that the city began to take its Homeric form in the late Bronze Age (*c.* 1500 BCE). After being severely damaged by an earthquake in about 1300 BCE, the city was rebuilt, only to fall again to an attack in about 1190 BCE – perhaps the war described by Homer.

Archeological evidence for the historical truth of the Trojan War includes charred wood and rubble, human skeletons trapped indoors and covered with debris, skulls crushed by stones, a bronze arrowhead and, most tellingly, piles of stones that would have been hurled by slings during combat.

RECENT EVIDENCE

The main argument against associating these ruins with Homer's Troy is that the hill that was originally excavated contains the remains of a city too small and insignificant to be worth fighting over. However, recent excavations by a team led by German archeologist Manfred Korfmann of the University of Tübingen have overcome this objection. Korfmann's work has produced evidence that Troy was indeed a large and important city. Because of its strategic location, it could control sea access from the Aegean to the Black Sea through the Dardanelles Strait. New excavations have also verified the existence of a lower town, south and east of the citadel, making Homer's Troy about 15 times larger than had previously been believed.

Above The fortification walls of Troy protected the citadel or high city, which contained the royal palaces, temples and homes of the nobility. Evidence indicates that the walls were strengthened and repaired many times over the centuries.

'Troy is a complex layer cake of cities built one on top of another.'

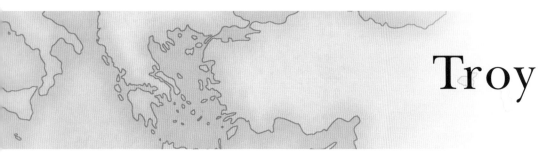

Troy

Important recent finds at the site of Troy have provided clues as to what the city must have looked like in the late Bronze Age. Based on plans and photographs from the actual dig, graphic artists are able to create three-dimensional computer reconstructions of the city.

Reconstruction is also aided by artistic representations – for instance, a Bronze Age domestic scene depicted on a painted vase. In the case of Homer's Troy, comparisons to better-preserved sites from the same time period, such as Mycenae and Akrotiri, also provide guidance. Though a reconstruction may be a work of the imagination, at its best it synthesizes everything that archeologists know about a place and gives people today the chance to imagine living there.

Since 1998, more than 350 scholars, scientists and technicians from over 20 countries have collaborated on excavations at the site under the direction of German archeologist Manfred Korfmann. Although Korfmann died in 2005, the work of Project Troia continues.

① CITADEL

Troy's citadel or acropolis (high city) was large for its time and surrounded by thick stone walls. Though the centre of the citadel was destroyed more than 2,000 years ago, the citadels of other late Bronze Age cities such as Mycenae provide important clues. Like Mycenae, Troy's citadel was probably a heavily fortified royal and religious compound, featuring monumental architecture. Within the walls were the residences of the royal family, the nobility and their household and staff, as well as one or more sanctuaries.

② TEMPLE OF ATHENA

The sanctuaries on the citadel were probably wooden buildings housing religious treasures. According to many ancient sources, among them was the Palladium – a wooden statue of the goddess Athena said to have fallen from heaven. Tradition held that as long as the Palladium remained at Troy, the city was safe. In the *Iliad*, Greek heroes Odysseus and Diomedes steal the Palladium, leaving Troy vulnerable to attack from Greek warriors hiding inside the wooden Trojan Horse, which the Trojans themselves haul within the citadel's gates. Existence of an earlier temple that housed the Palladium can be inferred from remains of a Classical temple to Athena built on the site during Greek and Roman times.

③ FORTIFICATION WALL

Archeologists have uncovered remains of the fortification wall that surrounded the citadel. Evidence of repeated

repairs to the wall, and attempts to enlarge and strengthen it, indicate that Troy was often attacked.

④ UPPER TOWN

Inside the citadel, large houses belonging to the nobles of Troy lined the inside of the fortification wall. Though stone from houses belonging to the various levels of Troy was reused in later construction, gaps in the archeological record can be filled in by looking at buildings found elsewhere in Troy and at comparable sites. Archeologists believe that one style of house on the citadel may have had stone pillars supporting the upper floor and roof of a large open hall.

⑤ LOWER TOWN

Archeological evidence now shows that from the 17th to the early 12th centuries BCE, the city of Troy spread beyond the citadel's fortification wall to include a lower settlement to the south and east. The settled area stretched 400 metres (1,300 feet) south of the citadel and housed 5,000–10,000 people. Conclusions about the layout of the lower town are based on trial trenches and excavations undertaken since 1993, including a systematic pottery survey in 2003.

⑥ LOWER-TOWN DWELLINGS

Houses in the lower town were built of stone and mud bricks, as can be surmised from remains and from modern houses near Troy that have been built using materials and techniques available in the past. Archeologists speculate that the residents of the lower town were artisans and merchants who supported the citadel. A unique feature of Homeric Troy is the pithoi (pottery vessels) used to store wine, olive oil and grain. Remains of these vessels have been found sunk into the floors of houses and covered with stones. Some archeologists believe this practice suggests that residents had a 'siege mentality' and lived in expectation of future attacks.

⑦ DEFENSIVE DITCH WITH INNER PALISADE

The residential areas of the lower town outside the citadel's fortification wall were protected by lighter fortifications. Surveys and excavations since 1993 have shown that the lower city was surrounded, at least in the 13th century BCE, by a U-shaped fortification ditch, 3.5 metres (11½ feet) wide and 2 metres (6½ feet) deep carved into the limestone bedrock. This ditch may have protected the city from attacks from horse-drawn war chariots – new and dangerous weapons during the Bronze Age. A few metres inside the main ditch is a shallower ditch, which suggests that there was also an inner fence or palisade, probably made of wood.

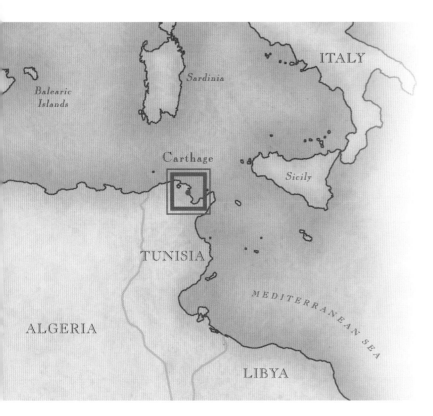

Carthage – North African superpower

Originally settled by Phoenician colonists, Carthage grew into a commercial and military superpower that challenged the Roman Empire for dominance of the Mediterranean during the 2nd and 3rd centuries BCE. The city was located on a promontory near modern-day Tunis in Tunisia, a strategic site from which it could control ships passing through the Mediterranean.

Rivalry with Rome led to a series of wars – known as the Punic Wars – each of which Carthage lost. Although the story of the founding of Carthage contains legendary elements, the essence of the story is supported by archeological evidence.

QUEEN DIDO

According to the Greek historian Timaeus (*c.* 345–*c.* 250 BCE), Carthage was founded in 814 BCE by a Phoenician princess known as Dido (Elissa in Phoenician). After the death of her powerful husband at the hand of her ambitious brother, Dido fled from her home in Tyre, a Phoenician city in Lebanon, and bargained with a local ruler for land in North Africa upon which to build a new city (*Carthage* means 'new city' in Phoenician). The original bargain granted Dido as much land as an ox-hide could cover. Dido cleverly cut the ox-hide into strips and laid them end-to-end, outlining the site of her city.

According to the *Aeneid*, the Latin epic written by Virgil in the 1st century BCE, Dido offered asylum to Aeneas, a son of King Priam, after the fall of Troy and he became her lover. When Aeneas deserted Dido to fulfil his divinely appointed mission of founding the city of Rome, Dido swore vengeance on the descendants of Troy (creating the mythic causes for the Punic Wars) and killed herself with Aeneas' sword.

DEFEAT OF A POWERFUL CITY

At its height in the 4th century BCE Carthage was one of the largest cities in the world, containing markets, towers, a theatre, a circus (racetrack) and four large residential districts. Modern estimates place the city's population at more than 250,000.

Carthage had two large harbours, one for its more than 300 war galleys and the other for trading vessels. Merchant ships from Carthage imported and distributed tin from Cornwall (which was used to make bronze) and silver from mines in Iberia, such as those at Tartessos (see pages 38–39). Carthage also exported textiles, including cloth dyed with valuable 'Tyrian Purple', a dye formula worth 15–20 times its weight in gold. In addition it manufactured and traded a wide variety of other goods, including furniture, armaments, jewellery, wine, olive oil and household products.

Though Rome was a trading partner of Carthage, the city's aggressive dominance soon became a threat to Roman power in the region. Three wars waged between the two empires between 265 and 146 BCE altered the course of Western civilization. In the second Punic War (218–201 BCE) the Carthaginian general Hannibal marched an army, including war elephants, from Iberia (modern Spain) over the Pyrenees and the Alps into northern Italy. He defeated Rome in a number of battles, but lacked the military strength to attack the city of Rome itself. The third Punic War (149–146 BCE) ended in the complete defeat of Carthage. The victorious Romans burned Carthage's warships in its harbour, slaughtered or enslaved its people and set the city ablaze.

'At its height in the 4th century BCE, Carthage was one of the largest cities in the world.'

Right The temple columns atop Byrsa Hill, with a grand view over the Gulf of Tunis, are remains of Carthage, a beautiful and wealthy ancient sea port destroyed by the Romans in 146 BCE.

ANCIENT TRAGEDY

In the 20th century, archeologists found evidence of a ritual practice that had made Carthage notorious in the ancient world. Since 1921, when the site was discovered, archeological work has continued at the Carthage necropolis or cemetery, which contains an estimated 20,000 burial urns with the charred remains of young animals and children, almost certainly sacrifices to win special favours from the gods.

The cult of child sacrifice at Carthage is described in terrible detail in the writings of Greek and Roman historians. One such account says that a child would be placed in the outstretched hands of a bronze statue of the city's deity, from where the victim would roll down into a pit filled with fire! Though a few modern historians have argued that the children buried in the necropolis may have died of natural causes, or that their deaths were a primitive way of regulating population growth, most agree that the cities of Meso-America were not alone in practising ritual human sacrifice.

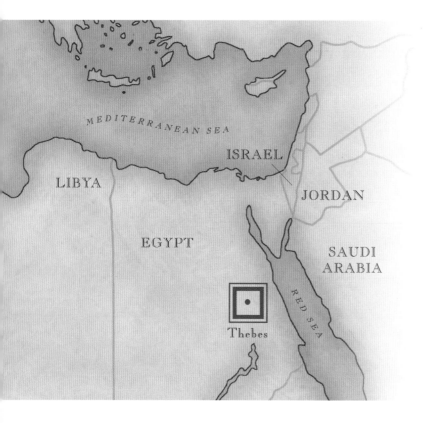

Thebes – city of pharaohs

The capital of Egypt during two dynasties, Thebes is a spectacular city of ancient temples and tombs. On the east bank of the Nile stands the great temple complex of Karnak. On the west bank is the Valley of the Kings, with the tombs of 64 of Egypt's New Kingdom pharaohs. It is here that the most famous discovery of modern archeology was made, when Howard Carter opened the tomb of King Tutankhamun.

Excavations are still under way at the site, and newly rediscovered tombs are revealing their secrets.

TEMPLES AND TOMBS

The temple complex of Karnak in Thebes is the largest ancient religious site in the world. Construction began during the 16th century BCE, but about 30 pharaohs contributed to the buildings. The largest temple is dedicated to Amun-Re, the Egyptian creator god. Smaller temples and chapels are dedicated to Mut, consort of Amun-Re, and their son Montu, a war god, as well as to a number of other gods. Karnak's Hypostyle Hall, which is considered an architectural masterpiece, was started by Ramesses I, who founded the 19th Egyptian dynasty but ruled for only one year (1295–1294 BCE). The Hypostyle Hall was completed by his successors Seti I (1294–1279 BCE) and Ramesses II (1279–1213 BCE). (All dates given for pharaohs refer to the approximate years they ruled.) The lofty roof of the Hall, 25 metres (82 feet) high, is supported by stately rows of sandstone columns and its walls are carved with reliefs. The southern

walls have hieroglyphic texts recording details of a peace treaty between Ramesses II and a Hittite king.

The Valley of the Kings was used for royal burials from about 1539 to 1075 BCE. The tombs of pharaohs from Thutmose I (1504–1492 BCE) to Ramesses XI (1102–1069 BCE) are located here, as well as tombs of many of their wives, children and favourite nobles. Some of the tombs have been open since Classical times; the tomb of Ramesses IV features graffiti carved in Greek and Latin by ancient tourists. Other tombs have been excavated only recently.

MILESTONES OF REDISCOVERY

The earliest modern explorers of Thebes were scholars who arrived in Egypt with Napoleon's invasion force in 1799. Unlike many other visitors, who were less interested in scholarship than in collecting antiquities, Napoleon's expedition made an effort to document its findings, publishing maps and plans of Thebes' temples and tombs. However, serious Egyptology could not begin until French archeologist Jean-François Champollion, who visited the Valley in 1829,

deciphered the hieroglyphic alphabet, enabling researchers to read the inscriptions on the monuments.

The most celebrated rediscovery in the Valley is the tomb of Tutankhamun (ruled 1333–1323 BCE), a minor pharaoh of the 18th dynasty. When British archeologist Howard Carter opened the tomb on 26 November 1922 he made a sensational discovery. The tomb had not been plundered and was filled with treasures, including the young king's golden funeral mask and a priceless collection of statues, containers, jewellery and ornaments made of gold, alabaster, ivory and other precious materials, adorned with scarabs, cloisonné and gems.

In 1995 archeologists from the Theban Mapping Project (TMP) – an international team based at the American University in Cairo, who were preparing a comprehensive database of Thebes' thousands of tombs and temples – rediscovered what has proved to be the largest tomb in the valley. Though the entrance to the tomb was first noted by British archeologist James Burton in 1825, it was so choked with debris that Burton was able to enter only the first nine chambers. After clearing the debris, TMP investigators under the direction of Professor Kent R. Weeks opened a path into the tomb's interior and found at least 130 corridors and chambers with decorated walls and hundreds of potsherds, beads and amulets. Hieroglyphic texts on the walls identified the tomb as the original burial place of several sons of Ramesses II.

PRESENT-DAY EXPLORATION

The most recently opened chamber in the Valley promised at first to be a major discovery. In March 2005 a team from the University of Memphis in Tennessee, under the direction of Egyptologist Otto Schaden, opened a new tomb chamber that contained seven wooden coffins and several large storage jars. However, rather than mummies and rich burial goods, the coffins contained mummification supplies, including salts, linens and broken pottery.

In February 2006, it was announced that the University of Memphis team had found a new tomb, about 25 metres (82 feet) south of the tomb of Tutankhamun. The burial chamber held seven wooden human-shaped coffins with painted faces as well as pottery jars and other materials.

Below There are 134 impressive columns at the Temple of Amun complex. Reliefs carved into the interior and exterior walls depict ceremonial processions and military victories as well as stories from Egyptian mythology.

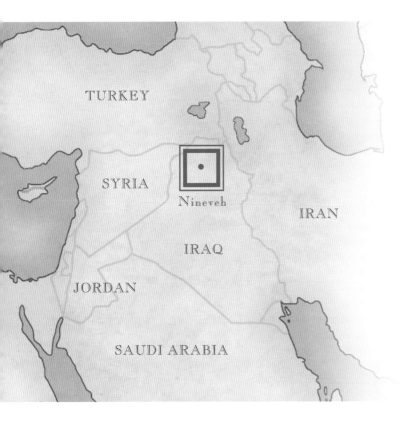

Nineveh – stronghold of Assyrian kings

Nineveh, an important city in ancient Assyria, dates back to biblical times. The ruins lie just outside Mosul in Iraq, on the banks of the Tigris River. It is the 'exceedingly great city of three days journey' (a circuit of perhaps 100 km or 60 miles) that Jonah was fleeing when he was swallowed by the whale for disobeying God's request to preach to its sinful inhabitants.

Right *Nineveh was a large city surrounded by imposing stone walls with 15 great gates. As many as 100,000 people lived inside these walls, making Nineveh among the largest urban settlements of its time.*

Though Nineveh dates back to 1800 BCE, when it was known as a sacred place of the goddess Ishtar, the city owed its grandeur to the lavish palaces and temples constructed by its kings. Between about 880 and 630 BCE, Nineveh was the stronghold and capital city of a series of great and powerful Assyrian kings, including Sennacherib, who conquered many cities in Judah and laid siege to Jerusalem itself.

ROYAL CONSTRUCTION

Sennacherib, Nineveh's most famous king who ruled between 701 and 681 BCE, enlarged the city, adding wide boulevards, large squares, parks and gardens as well as monumental palaces and public buildings. Sennacherib also built bridges and dug an elaborate system of canals and aqueducts to bring water from the hills.

He also constructed the city's walls, 12 km (7½ miles) in circumference, with 15 great

gates, each named after an Assyrian god. Some of the gates were guarded by pairs of winged bulls, and the walls themselves were decorated with bas-relief carvings. The enclosed area was home to more than 100,000 people, making Nineveh among the largest cities of the world in its day.

Sennacherib's most impressive building project was the 'palace without a rival' that the king commissioned for himself. It had overall dimensions of approximately 210 by 200 metres (680 by 650 feet), boasted a total of 27 entrances and 80 halls and rooms. The palace's main doorways were guarded by statues of giant animals, such as winged bulls with human heads and bronze lions. Many of its rooms had glazed brick panelling and were adorned with huge stone slabs carved in relief with images of Sennacherib's military victories. On the colossal statue at the doorway of the throne room is a cuneiform inscription giving Sennacherib's own account of his unsuccessful siege of Jerusalem in 701 BCE, which differs from the biblical story in 2 Kings.

Seventy years later, in about 633 BCE, Nineveh was substantially weakened by an attack from the Medes, an ancient people from northern Persia. The city was attacked again in 625 BCE by an alliance of the Medes and Babylonians, who succeeded in conquering Nineveh in 612 BCE, razing its monuments. People who could not escape to other Assyrian cities were massacred or captured and deported, and the victorious Medes and Babylonians divided Nineveh's lands between them.

ARCHEOLOGICAL DIGS

The remains of Nineveh were discovered in the early 19th century, when the French consul at Mosul began to explore two

mounds situated across the Tigris River from the central city. The excavation soon uncovered the remains of the royal palace that had been constructed by Sargon II, the father of Sennacherib. Then, in 1849, a young British adventurer called Sir Austen Henry Layard rediscovered the palace of Sennacherib. Considering that the palace had been sacked and burned during the fall of Nineveh, its walls and their relief sculptures were found to be surprisingly well preserved. Layard also located the library of Nineveh's King Ashurbanipal (ruled 669–626 BCE), which contained some 22,000 inscribed clay tablets.

Subsequent excavations undertaken by archeologists connected to various European museums rediscovered palaces built by Nineveh's other kings, along with sculpted slabs detailing the life, customs and beliefs of the city's people. Among the most important finds were more than 300 fragments of 'prisms' – six-sided baked clay documents on which Nineveh's kings recorded their achievements. The Taylor Prism, now in the British Museum in London, is intact. It records details from Sennacherib's first eight military campaigns, including his destruction of 46 cities in Judah and the deportation of more than 200,000 people.

NINEVEH TODAY

In the 1960s, recognizing that the ruins of Sennacherib's palace were a national treasure, the Iraq Department of Antiquities roofed the site and turned it into a museum. However, security there has been notably lax, and numerous looted fragments of Assyrian reliefs from the palace have been bought and sold on the antiquities market, completing the work of destruction begun by the Medes and Babylonians.

'Nineveh is the "exceedingly great city" that Jonah was fleeing when he was swallowed by the whale.'

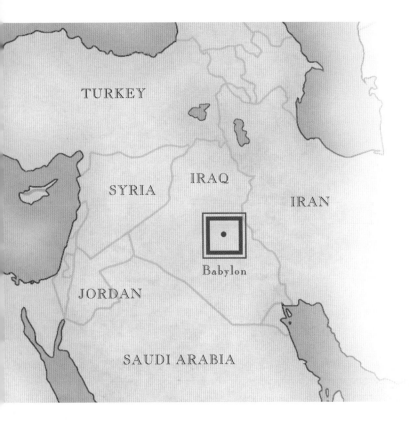

TURKEY

SYRIA

IRAQ

IRAN

Babylon

JORDAN

SAUDI ARABIA

Babylon – city of fallen empires

Babylon, a city on the Euphrates River in ancient Mesopotamia, today about 100 km (60 miles) south of Baghdad in Iraq, has been ruled by many powerful empires since the days of its first great king, Hammurabi (ruled 1792–1750 BCE). Since that time Babylon has been conquered many times, and its monuments have been repeatedly destroyed and rebuilt.

During the 6th century BCE, Babylon was rebuilt by King Nebuchadnezzar into a magnificent city, which was then conquered by the Persian Empire. In 1982 Saddam Hussein constructed a lavish palace for himself over the ruins of Babylon, until he too was toppled from power.

HAMMURABI AND THE TOWER OF BABEL

Though references to Babylon date back to the 3rd millennium BCE, its first great king was Hammurabi. He built Babylon's first ziggurat or temple tower, probably the inspiration for the Tower of Babel, said in the book of Genesis to have been built by the descendants of Noah so that its top would reach to heaven. The divine punishment for this presumption is said to be the world's many languages.

Under Hammurabi, Babylon was one of the largest cities in the world and was renowned for its laws and learning. Inscribed in cuneiform on a black stela found in the ruins of Susa, where it had been taken by the Elamites who conquered Babylon in about 1600 BCE, is the Code of

Hammurabi – a detailed series of civic laws and their punishments as well as guidelines for settling common disputes and rules for proper civic conduct. Hammurabi's Babylon was also noted for its sophisticated literature and its scholarship in medicine, mathematics, astronomy and other sciences.

FALLEN EMPIRES

Following the death of Hammurabi, Babylon fell into decline and, over the next 1,000 years, was conquered by a series of empires, including those of the Hittites and the Assyrians. In *c.* 689 BCE the Assyrian king Sennacherib destroyed the city, razing its walls, temples and palaces to the ground.

Right *Decorating Babylon's Ishtar Gate are blue glazed tiles with alternating rows of bas-relief sirrush (dragons), such as the one shown here, and aurochs, an extinct kind of cattle.*

In 625 BCE, the Babylonian king Nabopolassar (ruled 625–605 BCE) formed an alliance with the Medes, a people of what is now western Iran, and fought back against the Assyrians, finally destroying their capital Nineveh in 612. With Assyria eliminated, the Babylonian Empire controlled all the lands from the Tigris River to the Mediterranean.

Under Nebuchadnezzar II (Nabopolassar's son, who ruled 604–562 BCE), the city of Babylon reached its greatest glory. Nebuchadnezzar expanded the city into a splendid capital for his Chaldean or New Babylonian Empire. He doubled the city's size, built massive walls and ornamental gates, restored the Temple of Marduk (the

To the dismay of archeologists, in 1985 Saddam Hussein started rebuilding Babylon on top of its ruins. Imitating Nebuchadnezzar, he stamped many of the bricks used in the reconstruction with his own name. He also constructed a lavish palace overlooking the Euphrates River. Shaped like a ziggurat, the palace was decorated with marble and featured arched gates, towers and murals depicting scenes from ancient Babylon. The palace was never occupied and, like Babylon's previous rulers, Saddam Hussein fell from power when Iraq was occupied by US-led forces in 2003. Unfortunately a military base established near the ruins by American forces has led to further damage to this important archeological site.

Above *The Ishtar Gate was originally the eighth gate to the Inner City of Babylon. It was constructed on the north side of the city in about 575 BCE by order of King Nebuchadnezzar II.*

chief god of the city) and built himself a magnificent palace ornamented, some say, by the famous Hanging Gardens, which Greek historian Herodotus described as one of the seven wonders of the ancient world.

The story of Marduk – divine model for Nebuchadnezzar and all Babylonian kings – is told in the creation epic, the *Enuma Elish*. Recorded on seven clay tablets in the ancient Akkadian language, the myth dates back to the 8th century BCE. After an epic battle, the hero Marduk slays the female sea monster Tiamat and creates the world from her corpse. During the reign of Nebuchadnezzar, the *Enuma Elish* was recited annually at the New Year festival in celebration of Marduk as king of the gods and of Nebuchadnezzar's divinely ordained power and authority.

Nevertheless, Babylon was conquered again in 539 BCE, falling to Cyrus the Great

and the Persian Empire. As a Persian administrative capital, Babylonian arts and learning again flourished. However, the city eventually fell into decline, and in 331 BCE it was conquered again – this time by Alexander the Great. Alexander himself died mysteriously in the palace of Nebuchadnezzar in 323 BCE, and Babylon once again fell into desolation and ruin.

Babylon

The Babylon of Nebuchadnezzar II was not a new city but already had a long history, dating back at least 2,000 years. Over that time, the city had been ruled by many kings. Some built monuments to their accomplishments, while others, like the Assyrian conqueror Sennacherib, razed the city's buildings and dumped the rubble into the Euphrates River.

Unlike his predecessors, Nebuchadnezzar did not simply restore Babylon's historic temples and palaces. Rather, he built a new capital city as a reflection of his royal authority. A verse quoting Nebuchadnezzar in the book of Daniel (4:30) makes this purpose clear: 'Is not this Babylon, which I have built by my mighty power as a royal residence and for the glory of my majesty?'. The city's size and its huge walls, palaces and temples made it an icon of imperial power.

Until the rise of imperial Rome, Babylon was the largest city in the Mediterranean region. Greek writers, even those who had never seen it, were impressed by its extent. Aristotle described it as 'a city that has the circuit of a nation rather than a city'. Built in the flat expanse of the Euphrates River valley, the city's towering walls and ziggurat would have been visible from a great distance. Herodotus, who may have travelled there, marvelled that its walls were 'fifty royal cubits wide and two hundred cubits high'.

The Euphrates and the moats around the walls made the city look like it was rising out of the waters. Scholars have interpreted this as a reference to the myth of the creation of the world by Marduk after his defeat of Tiamat (see page 129). Babylon, the city's layout seemed to say, is the place where creation rises from the sea, where heaven and earth are joined so human beings can live.

① EUPHRATES RIVER

One of Asia's largest rivers, the Euphrates is 2,720 km (1,700 miles) long. The Bible refers to it as the 'great river' and says that it was one of the four rivers that flowed out of the Garden of Eden. Some of the great battles of history took place along the Euphrates, including the defeat of the Egyptian Pharaoh Necho II by King Nebuchadnezzar II in 605 BCE, a battle that is mentioned several times in the Bible.

② WALLS

Under Nebuchadnezzar, Babylon was enclosed in massive walls. According to the Greek historian Herodotus, the walls were broad enough at the top for two horse-drawn chariots to meet and pass. The Inner City was also enclosed by walls constructed of sun-dried brick. Though less imposing than the city's outer defences, the city's inner walls created a sense of order and emphasized the importance of the temples and monuments that they enclosed.

③ PROCESSION STREET

The city's central thoroughfare, called Procession Street, was 19 metres (63 feet) wide and paved with red and white stone slabs. Lining the street on both sides for about 200 metres (650 feet) were two high walls decorated with blue ceramic tiles depicting 120 bas-reliefs of lions striding forward, emblems of the goddess Ishtar. This walled portion of the street led to the magnificent Ishtar Gate, one of the entrances to Babylon's Inner City. From there, the street led directly to the Temple of Marduk, also called the Esagila Temple.

④ ISHTAR GATE

The magnificent Ishtar Gate was covered with dark blue tiles depicting about 150 dragons and bulls, symbols of the gods Marduk and Adad, protectors of the city. At the New Year festival, a statue of Marduk was carried through the gate to the temple, reconfirming the king's divine authority. The German archeologists who excavated Babylon in the 19th century shipped material from the gate back to Germany so that it could be reconstructed in the Pergamon Museum in Berlin as a symbol of the accomplishments of the ancient world.

⑤ INNER CITY

At Babylon's heart was the rectangular Inner City, the site of its most imposing monuments. These including the main sanctuary of Babylon – the Esagila temple with its massive ziggurat, the Etemenanki, dedicated to Marduk, the chief god of the city. Two walls and a moat surrounded the Inner City, and the city's major streets led to this central location.

⑥ ESAGILA TEMPLE

Also called the Temple of Marduk, this massive building created an impression of overwhelming power. Built from clay, heavily bastioned and with huge square towers and crenellated terraces, the building looked more like a fort than a house of worship.

⑦ ETEMENANKI

The ziggurat, called in Sumerian the Etemenanki (which means 'foundation platform of heaven and underworld'), was built originally by Hammurabi and stood about 100 metres (328 feet) tall. It is thought to be the source for the Tower of Babel story. According to Herodotus, it had eight levels (scholars now believe that there were seven) with an external pathway that could be ascended on foot. He reports that on the summit there was a great temple with gold furnishings, which no one could enter except a priestess chosen by the god Marduk.

⑧ HANGING GARDENS

Nebuchadnezzar II is also credited with Babylon's Hanging Gardens, which Herodotus called one of the wonders of the ancient world. Legend says they were built for the king's wife, Amyitus of Media, who longed for the trees and plants of her homeland. Though Greek sources describe the terraced gardens, and excavations in the early 20th century by German archeologist Robert Koldewey were thought to reveal their foundations, archeologists today are not certain whether the gardens were located in Babylon or in Nineveh.

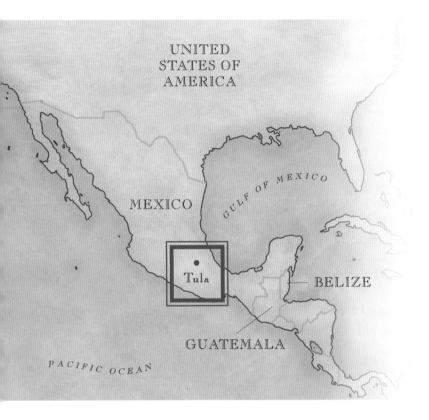

Tula – city of Quetzalcóatl

Stories of the ancient Toltecs of Tula are found in the oral and written histories of many peoples from central Mexico. Even the Aztecs held the Toltecs in high regard, believing them to be an admirable, noble and very accomplished people. Much of the Toltecs' renown can be traced to the stories associated with their most famous king, Topiltzin, who took the name Quetzalcóatl when he assumed the kingship.

Although legends about Quetzalcóatl ('Feathered Serpent') had been told in Mexico since the 1st millennium BCE, it was in Tula that the god became humanized as a renowned builder and priestly king.

QUETZALCÓATL'S CAPITAL

The ruins of the ancient capital of the Toltecs are located near the colonial city of Tula in central Mexico, about 100 km (60 miles) north-west of Mexico City. Ancient Tula flourished between the 10th and mid-12th centuries, before the rise of Aztec city-states like Tenochtitlan. At its height, Tula was home to an ethnically diverse population of 30,000–40,000 people.

Native documents, such as the Aztec Codex Chimpalpopoca, describe Tula as a magnificent city filled with terraced pyramids, colonnaded walkways and artisans' workshops. Residential streets were laid out in a grid, and there were two large courts for playing the Meso-American ball game, a sport with ritual associations. The city's main plaza was flanked by two impressive pyramids elaborately decorated with carved reliefs of prowling jaguars, eagles, rattlesnakes and

other animals of prey. Statues of large reclining figures known as *chacmools*, characteristic of Tula, were later copied by Aztec sculptors who wanted to align themselves with the artistry of the Toltecs.

These accounts also say that Tula's farmers raised cotton, maize, squash and amaranth plants of exceptional size. Treasure collected by the Toltecs as tribute from vassal cities was stored in special houses, including a golden house, a seashell house, a turquoise house and a house of precious feathers, the most precious of which were the iridescent green-gold and blue-violet feathers of the Resplendent Quetzal – a spectacular tropical bird.

TULA'S LEGENDARY RULER

The history of Tula has become intertwined with myths about Quetzalcóatl – the mythical culture hero from whom almost all Meso-American peoples claim descent. In Nahuatl, the indigenous language of central Mexico, *quetzalli* means 'long green feather' and *coatl* means 'snake'. In assuming the name Quetzalcóatl, Tula's founding king elevated himself to godly status and established a

WHAT HAPPENED TO TULA?

Archeologists have been trying to reconstruct the history of Tula and its connection to later Mayan cities such as Chichen Itza since the late 1800s. Whatever happened to Quetzalcóatl, the ruins indicate that Tula fell around the middle of the 12th century, probably as a result of war between rival ethnic groups. Because of these disputes and a prolonged drought, people migrated away from Tula. Soon war broke out in the weakened city. Major buildings were burned, monuments destroyed and archeologists have uncovered skeletal remains of people who were killed in battle.

model of conduct for rulers. The narrative of Quetzalcóatl's exile from the city of Tula probably combines actual historical details with elements of mythic, religious and cosmological symbolism.

According to legend, disputes arose during the mid-12th century between Tula's diverse ethnic factions. One faction favoured Quetzalcóatl, a priestly king who was the champion of arts and culture and was said to sacrifice only serpents, birds and butterflies. The other faction favoured Tezcatlipoca – a war-like shamanic wizard who demanded human sacrifice. The story goes that Tezcatlipoca tricked Quetzalcóatl into getting drunk on fermented cactus juice. While drunk, Quetzalcóatl committed incest with his sister. Overcome with remorse, he withdrew from power and exiled himself from Tula with a band of followers.

There are several versions of what happened next. In one version, many of Quetzalcóatl's followers froze to death on a snowy mountain pass, and Quetzalcóatl journeyed on alone to the Gulf of Mexico. In another, Quetzalcóatl, dressed in precious feather garments and a turquoise mask, set himself on fire and rose from the funeral pyre as the morning star. Another version has him setting sail on a raft of woven serpents, promising to return.

Yet another tradition says that because Quetzalcóatl thought his face was ugly, he let his beard grow to cover it and eventually wore a white mask. This version gave rise to the now-discredited idea that the Aztec king Motecuhzoma opened his city to Hernán Cortés because he believed this bearded white man was Quetzalcóatl returning to his people, as he had promised.

Above *Made from assembled drum-like segments, the colossal warrior columns at the top of Pyramid B at Tula announce that the structure was the seat of supreme authority in the ancient city.*

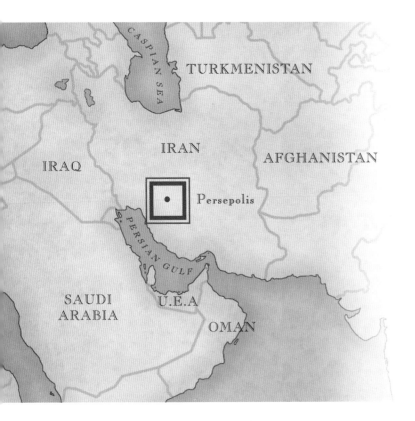

Persepolis – city of ancient Iran

Persepolis was founded by Darius the Great, king of the second Persian dynasty (often called the Achaemenid Empire), around 518 BCE. The ruins are located about 70 km (44 miles) north-east of the modern city of Shiraz in Iran. The ancient Persians called the city Parsa, which means 'city of the Persians'; the Greek name, Persepolis, has the same meaning. Darius designed his capital city's monumental palaces, gates and pillared halls as a show place for receptions and festivals.

The city's spectacular natural setting, on a plain rimmed by purple cliffs, gives Persepolis an imposing imperial feel.

DARIUS THE GREAT

As the successor to the war-like king Cyrus the Great, who succeeded in conquering Babylon in 539 BCE, Darius also led his army on battles of conquest, including successful campaigns to expand his empire into India and Europe and an attack on the Greek mainland, which resulted in his defeat at the Battle of Marathon in 490 BCE. But the accomplishments for which Darius is most lauded are the practical ways he improved everyday life in his empire, establishing within a reign of 36 years a government that became an ancient model of organization and efficiency.

Darius divided the empire into 20 provinces, each under the supervision of a local governor or *satrap*, and allowed each province to retain its laws and traditions. He also commissioned an extensive network of roads, dug a canal from the Nile to Suez so that ships could reach Persia via the Red Sea, established a postal system, standardized weights and measures, developed a system of coinage and promoted scholarship and religious tolerance. But the project for which Darius is most remembered is the construction of the new ceremonial capital of Persepolis. Though work on the capital's buildings and monuments continued through the reign of his son Xerxes I (485–465 BCE), it was Darius who laid out the city and began the construction of its most impressive monuments.

THE RISE AND FALL OF PERSEPOLIS

The art and architecture of Persepolis, with its well-organized site plan and rich decoration, celebrate the idea that Darius had given his empire's diverse people a unified identity. The materials and the artisans who built the city came from every corner of the empire – stone-cutters from Ionia, cedar trees from Lebanon, gold from Sardis, goldsmiths from Medea, ivory from Ethiopia, silver and ebony from Egypt. Though the decorative style was eclectic, Darius never lost sight of his own unifying role and importance. His elegant Audience Hall, supported by 72 tall pillars, bears the inscription: 'Darius the great king, king of kings, king of countries, son of Hystaspes, an Achaemenian, built this palace.' Another

'Darius the great king, king of kings, king of countries, son of Hystaspes, an Achaemenian, built this palace.'

inscription expresses the great king's satisfaction with what he had constructed: 'I built it secure and beautiful and adequate, just as I was intending to.'

The next two centuries saw the Achaemenid Empire flourish. Then fighting and assassinations among competitors for the throne weakened the empire, and in 330 BCE it was conquered by the most brilliant military strategist of the ancient world – Alexander the Great. Classical sources say that after occupying Persepolis, Alexander burned its palaces during a night of drunken revelry. Archeological evidence confirms that at least one of the palaces at Persepolis was destroyed by fire. At its height, the city was the wealthiest in the world, but most of its treasure was carted off by Alexander's army, a task that required 20,000 mules and 5,000 camels, according to the Greek historian Plutarch (c. 46–127 CE), who wrote a biography of Alexander.

REDISCOVERY AND EXCAVATION

The first scientific exploration of the ruins of Persepolis did not take place until the 1930s, though the site had been conclusively identified in the early 19th century when German scholar G.F. Grotefend deciphered cuneiform inscriptions on the ruins. In 1930 the Iranian government chose Ernst Herzfeld of the Oriental Institute of the University of Chicago to map, clear and excavate the site. Excavation continued throughout the 1930s, during which time many important structures, artworks and artefacts were uncovered and catalogued.

Darius and his successor kings helped archeologists to reconstruct the chronology of Persepolis by their practice of inscribing their names on the structures they built. Inscriptions written on foundation slabs, wall pegs and cylinder seals found in the ruins indicate which king was responsible for which structure. Xerxes added the following inscription to the Audience Hall built by Darius: 'When my father Darius went away from the throne, I became king on his throne by the grace of Ahuramazda. After I became king, I finished what had been done by my father, and I added other works.'

Below The Persepolitan Stairway was the main ceremonial entrance to the complex. The 111 steps of this broad double stair were built 7 metres (23 feet) wide to allow a horse and rider to mount them.

Persepolis

Persepolis was one of the most awe-inspiring cities of the ancient world. Its palaces and monuments were built on top of a vast platform, partly artificial and partly cut into a mountainside. The platform, known today as Persepolis Terrace, measures some 450 metres (1,475 feet) by 300 metres (985 feet) and is as much as 20 metres (65 feet) high.

On the east side of the terrace is Kuh-e Rahmet, the Mountain of Mercy. The other three sides are formed by a retaining wall. To create a level platform, workers filled depressions with soil and rocks and joined slabs with metal clips. Most of the buildings are built of dark grey limestone.

The terrace was reached by way of the grand Persepolitan Stairway, on the western side of the complex. At the top of the stairs was an impressive gate constructed by Xerxes. Visitors had to pass through this gate on their way to the Throne Hall to pay homage to the king. The gate consisted of an imposing hall supported by four stone columns. A pair of colossal winged bulls guard the western entrance, and two bulls with human heads stand at the eastern doorway. Engraved above each is an inscription in three languages stating that Xerxes built the gate. The widest doorway, on the south, leads to the Apadana.

The Apadana was the most magnificent structure at Persepolis. Begun by Darius and completed by Xerxes, it contains the enormous Audience Hall. Each side of the hall is 60.5 metres (198 feet) long, supported by 72 columns, 13 of which are still standing. The tops of the columns were decorated with many sculptures of bulls, lions and eagles.

Another important building was the Treasury, adjacent to the Throne Hall. This structure served both as a military armoury and as a royal storehouse. Many of the treasures stored within it had been brought back to Persepolis from conquered lands; the remainder came from annual tribute. Xerxes was so successful in his campaigns that in 476 BCE the Treasury employed 1,348 people, some of whom worked as 'gold and silver shiners'. A stone relief shows Darius on his throne, with Xerxes and other court officials behind him, accepting greetings from a high dignitary.

The Palace of Darius was another fine building, with a central hall supported by 12 columns. Reliefs on the stairways depict servants carrying food in covered dishes to be served at the king's table. Other reliefs show the king in formal dress leaving the palace, followed by his attendants.

The Harem of Xerxes contained the apartments for the queen and the court ladies. The central hall of the building had a portico facing a spacious courtyard to the north and scenes from palace life were carved to decorate the door jambs. One scene shows Xerxes entering the hall followed by two attendants, one carrying a fly whisk and the other holding a parasol over the king's head. Around the central hall were a number of individual apartments, each with a large pillared room and several smaller rooms.

① THRONE HALL

The Throne Hall was also called the Hall of a Hundred Columns. Supporting the massive roof were 72 wooden columns on stone bases, each 20 metres (65 feet) tall. There were 36 columns standing inside the hall and 36 more supported porticoes that lined three sides of the building. An inscription makes clear who built the hall: 'This audience hall with columns of stone was made by Artaxerxes, the great king. He, the son of king Darius, the Achaemenid, [says]: May Mithra protect me.' Today, 13 of the original columns are still standing.

② PLAZA OF ARMY

Outside the doors of the Throne Hall was the Plaza of Army, an assembly ground for troops. To the north of the plaza, the massive Army Gate, decorated by colossal sculptures of bulls, was under construction at the time the city was destroyed. The soldiers of Alexander the Great carried the wooden scaffolding that was being used for building the Army Gate across the Plaza of Army and stacked it in the halls of the Apadana so that the building's huge wooden beams would catch fire.

③ CEREMONIAL PROCESSION

Many delegations would have come to the Throne Hall to pay tribute to the king. Their magnificence can be judged from the beautiful reliefs that decorate the walls of the Apadana, depicting scenes from ceremonial processions. Carved in stone, delegates dressed in their native costumes and with characteristic headdresses, hairstyles and beards carry gifts of tribute to the king, including gold and silver vases, weapons, fabrics, jewellery and animals.

④ ANIMAL CAPITALS

The Throne Hall's columns were crowned by elaborate capitals. Each depicted two heads of a mighty animal like a bull or a lion. Between the two heads was a space where a wooden roof beam was supported. It is still possible to see traces of red paint on the throat of one of the lion heads on the capital of a column supporting the eastern portico.

'Many delegations came to the Throne Hall to pay tribute to the king.'

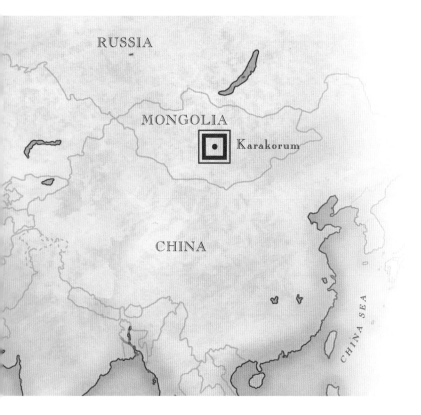

RUSSIA

MONGOLIA

Karakorum

CHINA

CHINA SEA

Karakorum – city of Genghis Khan

An important trading city on the Silk Road, Karakorum was the capital of the Mongol Empire of Genghis Khan in the 13th century. Archeological evidence indicates that Karakorum was a bustling cosmopolitan centre that drew people from across the Mongolian Empire, from Persia to China. Today the ruins lie on a grassy plain near the Orkhon River in north-central Mongolia.

Although the true capital of the empire was wherever the palatial yurt (Mongolian-style tent) of the empire's nomadic leader happened to be, the Khan and his court were in residence at Karakorum for some part of every year, and the city was the base for a garrison of Mongol fighters. After the death of Genghis Khan, Ögedei, the emperor's son and successor, built Karakorum into a true city.

MANUFACTURING AND TRADE

Situated along the most important east–west route across Mongolia, Karakorum was an ideal trading centre. Its most significant industry was metalwork. A canal brought water from the river to run bellows for forges that were used to make arrowheads, wheel bushings for carts and other useful and decorative metal objects. Archeological evidence also indicates that ceramics, glass beads for jewellery and yarn spun from the wool of sheep pastured on surrounding lands were also manufactured.

Trade, however, was Karakorum's lifeblood. Grain to supplement local produce was imported from China, as were decorative silk fabrics prized by the Mongols. Muslim merchants played a significant role in the city's economy, connecting Karakorum with cities in central Asia. China was also a significant trading partner; most of the coins that have been unearthed at Karakorum are of Chinese origin.

LAYOUT AND BUILDINGS

Much of what is known about Karakorum in the 13th century comes from the writings of a Franciscan monk, William de Rubruck, who visited Karakorum in the 1250s. He described the settlement as a mud-walled city with four entrance gates. Markets for a specific type of goods were located at each of these: horses were sold at the north gate, grain at the east gate, oxen and carts at the south gate and goats at the west gate. The city proper was divided into two principal districts. One was a Muslim commercial district surrounding the Khan's palace and the other contained the workshops and homes of Chinese artisans. There were also 12 temples of different nations, including several mosques and Buddhist temples and one Christian church.

The palace seems to have been used primarily for ceremonial purposes, such as receptions for ambassadors and two annual feasts, one in the spring on the Khan's eastward journey and one in late summer when he travelled back westwards. When he was in residence, the Khan probably set up his yurt on a large circular platform that has been found in the grounds. Yurts belonging to the Khan's entourage were erected outside the walls, swelling the city's year-round population of 10,000 people. The palace compound was a Chinese-style structure with a tiered roof. Remnants of ceramic roof tiles and finials (roof ornaments) have been discovered at the site.

The most spectacular feature of the palace was the Silver Tree fountain, designed by French artisan Guillaume Boucher. According to William de Rubruck, the fountain featured a central tree with silver branches, leaves and fruit, surrounded by four silver lions that dispensed four different beverages through a complex system of internal pipes: wine, mare's milk, honey drink and rice mead. At the top of the tree was an angel holding a trumpet.

COLLAPSE AND EXCAVATION

Karakorum's heyday was over quickly. In 1271 Kublai Khan established a new Mongol capital at Beijing, and Karakorum declined in importance. Over the next years, civil disturbances broke out in the city, and in 1388 the city was destroyed and the palace burned by Chinese soldiers from the Ming dynasty, who were pursuing the remnants of the Mongol army that they had expelled from China.

Although archeological excavations have been carried out at the site since the 1890s, much of Karakorum remains unexplored. Since 1999, a joint Mongolian-German archeological team has been working at Karakorum, primarily on the remains of the palace. Artefacts discovered include tile fragments, bricks, iron weapons, pottery, farming tools and copper coins. Porcelain fragments found at the site have been traced to production centres in China. Another unique discovery is a pharaoh's mask, which may have been offered for sale or presented as a gift to the Khan by a foreign visitor. Its presence testifies to Karakorum's far-reaching international connections.

Recent work at the site has also uncovered four round ovens that had been used for the purpose of baking roof tiles, bricks and other ornamental architectural materials. Researchers have concluded that the city's palace buildings featured decorative arches, floors of green ceramic tiles and roofs of red and green tiles. Remains show that the buildings were decorated with sculptures, painted figures and carvings.

'On the most important east–west route across Mongolia, Karakorum was an ideal trading centre.'

Below This ancient stone tortoise stands in front of Erdeni Dzu, a Buddhist monastery constructed near the ruins of Karakorum. The monastery is still active today.

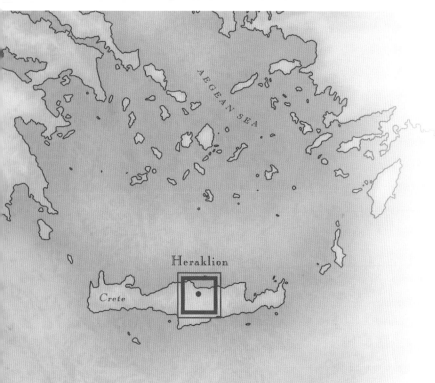

Knossos – labyrinth of King Minos

Minos was an ancient king who reigned over Crete and the islands of the Aegean Sea 300 years before the Trojan War. When Sir Arthur Evans conducted his famed excavations of the Bronze Age ruins near Heraklion in Crete, he called the civilization that he uncovered 'Minoan' and the complex of buildings that he excavated the 'Palace of King Minos'.

As later archeological work has affirmed, the buildings that were unearthed and partially restored by Evans were probably a central administrative or religious hub, around which a high civilization flourished between 1900 and 1400 BCE.

THE PALACE OF KING MINOS

As archeologists have discovered, there are five ancient palace complexes on Crete, but the one near Heraklion is the largest. Like Herakleion in Egypt, the city of Heraklion in Crete is named for the Greek hero Herakles (Hercules). The palace's four wings, which are arranged around a central courtyard, seem to have had an elaborate, maze-like structure. The 1,300 rooms, which included royal living quarters, workshops, shrines, storerooms, a theatre, an audience hall and a banqueting hall, were connected to each other by corridors of various lengths, suggesting to some historians the labyrinth in which King Minos imprisoned the Minotaur in Greek myth.

Life in the palace was comfortable. An elaborate system of terracotta pipes brought fresh water to fountains and taps. Other

Right A reconstructed sculpture of bull's horns has been placed among the ruins of the Royal Palace. The archeological work of Sir Arthur Evans was inspired by the tale of the Minotaur, the half-bull half-man monster who was imprisoned in a labyrinth on Crete.

WALL PAINTINGS

The walls of the palace were covered with art: mosaics and frescoes that depicted scenes of Minoan life. The frescoes show gentle activities, such as fishing and flower-gathering, as well as athletic feats, such as young men leaping over the backs of charging bulls. Fragments of painted pots, brightly coloured mosaics, delicate necklaces of bees and butterflies and urns decorated with flying dolphins attest to a culture of grace and elegance.

Perhaps the most famous artworks found at Knossos were two small glazed earthenware statues that represented a goddess, or perhaps her priestesses. One figure is wreathed in snakes; the other is holding a snake high in each hand. Their dresses have open bodices, leaving their breasts bare. One wears a flounced skirt with seven layers; a lion cub sits tamely on her head. Because they shed their skin and renew themselves, snakes have long been a symbol of death and regeneration, and this goddess is mistress of these natural cycles.

Right The reconstructed interior of the Royal Palace at Knossos shows the building's timbered ceiling and its stone and wood construction. Columns are made from tree trunks that were shaped, plastered and inserted upside down.

pipes carried away sewage. The queen's apartment had what was essentially a flush toilet, and an adjoining bathroom had a bath. Natural lighting and ceramic lamps burning olive oil provided illumination. In the storerooms, large clay pithoi (vases) held oil, grains, dried fish, beans and olives.

PEAK AND COLLAPSE

Minoan civilization reached its peak between 1600 and 1450 BCE when relations were established with Mycenae. People moved between Knossos and the citadel city in mainland Greece, which adopted Minoan culture as its own. Then, around 1500 BCE, the eruption of the volcanic island of Thera (Santorini), which buried Akrotiri, also sent earthquakes and tidal waves across the sea to Crete and shook the palaces to the ground. An invasion by the Dorian people around 1150 BCE brought the civilization to an end.

EXCAVATION AND RESTORATION

The first person to dig in the mound of archeological debris not far from Heraklion was Minos Kalokairinos, a local merchant and amateur archeologist. In 1878 he uncovered the foundations of storerooms filled with pithos jars. The first archeologist to try to buy the mound was the man who excavated Troy, Heinrich Schliemann. After Crete had won its independence, Sir Arthur Evans, an English amateur archeologist, used a family inheritance to buy the site. In 1900 he assembled a team of professional archeologists and local workers and began the excavation that uncovered the complex.

Evans' restorations and reconstructions are the most controversial aspects of his work. He used reinforced concrete rather than the materials of the time and his artists boldly re-created the frescoes from small fragments found in the ruins. Though the restorations may have been based on Evans' own interpretation of the ruins, he did make many significant finds, including about 3,000 tablets inscribed with text written in Linear A and Linear B script. The Linear B tablets date from a later occupation of the site by people from Mycenae. Those in Linear A that date back to Minoan times still remain largely undeciphered.

CHAPTER 6
SACRED CITIES

Cities can become sacred because important events in sacred history took place there, because they are the site of great temples and because, over the centuries, pilgrims have visited and venerated them. For instance, Teotihuacan, the great Meso-American city in the valley of Mexico, was regarded as sacred by the Aztecs because they associated its temples with their own creation myths. Similarly, Aksum, Ethiopia, gained sacred fame because legend says that the Ark of the Covenant was removed from Jerusalem and brought to Aksum by the son of the Queen of Sheba and King Solomon.

The great temples to the sun god Aten built by the Pharaoh Akhenaten sanctified his new capital city of Akhetaten. In the same way, the Classical temples to the Greek goddesses Hera and Athena at Paestum, Artemis at Ephesus and Aphrodite at Aphrodisias made their cities holy.

But most important, it is the faith and devotion of pilgrims that enriches and deepens a city's spiritual quality. Devotees of the Hindu god Shiva still flock to Vijayanagara's exquisite Virupaksha temple to celebrate annual festivals that mark events in the god's sacred biography.

Fabled cities of enlightenment and purity

The sacred cities of antiquity, such as those in this chapter, won their renown in different ways. Some became holy because they were sites of significant events in religious history or because they were connected to the life story of a sacred figure. For instance, the peaks around Takht-i-Suleiman, the pre-Islamic holy city in Iran, are connected with legends concerning the biblical King Solomon – Suleiman in Arabic.

Right *Teotihuacan was sacred to the Aztecs, who made frequent pilgrimages to its pyramids, including the impressive Pyramid of the Sun, shown here. Though the city had long been in ruins, the Aztecs regarded it as the source place of their own religious beliefs.*

At Epidauros, the famed healing city on the Greek Peloponnese, the Temple of Asklepios, the half-mortal Greek god of healing, is oriented to the east so that it faces Mount Titthion. This rounded hill is where the infant Asklepios was fed by a goat and guarded by the goatherd's dog in some versions of his myth.

Other cities were sites of important temples, shrines or places of worship, or functioned as the high seat of a particular religion. The Temple of Aphrodite in Aphrodisias and the Temple of Artemis in Ephesus, for example, were the most important shrines to these goddesses in Classical times. The city of Akhetaten and its temples to Aten, built by Middle Kingdom Pharaoh Akhenaten, was intended to replace Thebes as the seat of Egypt's state religion. Angkor Wat, the Hindu-Buddhist shrine in the forests of Cambodia, is the world's largest single religious monument.

In ancient times, sacred cities were often destinations for pilgrims and hosted religious festivals or annual rituals. The Aztecs, for instance, made frequent pilgrimages to the ruins of Teotihuacan, which they interpreted as the origin place of their own cosmology and mythology. Even today, ancient temples and sacred ruins continue to attract visitors, and religious festivals bring the holy cities of the past to life by filling them with today's seekers. Each April, Hindu pilgrims fill the ancient city of Vijayanagara for a festival that re-enacts the marriage of the god Shiva to Pampa, a beautiful local maiden.

To better understand how and why cities become sacred, let's look at two more familiar cities of enlightenment and purity. Bodhgaya in India, where the Buddha

Above *Aphrodisias, sacred city of Aphrodite, was once the site of the pre-eminent temple to the Greek goddess of love in Asia Minor. Set among cypress groves, the site was originally sacred to the ancient Mother Goddess.*

attained enlightenment, and Jerusalem, whose historic temples and shrines are sacred to three faiths, help us appreciate the power that the holy cities of antiquity had on the spiritual imaginations of the people of their time. Both cities continue to attract spiritual travellers, whose devotion adds new layers to the sanctity of these holy places.

BODHGAYA

The landscape and monuments of cities connected to the life story of an important spiritual figure are often imbued with a sacred meaning. Establishing a geographical location for sacred events helps to make religious stories feel more real, as well as providing a focus for the prayers of present-day believers.

The small city of Bodhgaya, in the north-eastern Indian province of Bihar, is filled with many temples and monuments that commemorate events in the spiritual biography of the Buddha. In the 5th century BCE Siddhartha Gautama, the Buddha-to-be, abandoned his life of privilege as an Indian prince and spent six years living with a small group of followers practising fasting and other spiritual austerities. Eventually, he realized that ascetic practices would not lead to the spiritual answers that he was seeking. Siddhartha accepted a drink of nourishing rice milk from a young girl. Thus fortified, Gautama sat down under a pipal tree and resolved not to move from his seat until he had reached the ultimate spiritual wisdom of enlightenment.

As the future Buddha sat in deep meditation, Mara, the Lord of Illusion, bombarded him with temptations and attacks. After three days and three nights of resisting these assaults through the power of his meditative concentration, the future Buddha's wisdom broke through Mara's illusions, the weapons of the attacking demons turned into flowers, and Siddhartha Gautama achieved the insight he had been seeking, becoming in that instant the Buddha, the enlightened one.

Since that time Bodhgaya has been revered as a holy city. In the 3rd century BCE the Buddhist emperor Ashoka (304–232 BCE) established a monastery and temple at the site of the Buddha's enlightenment. Known today as the Mahabodhi (Great Enlightenment) Temple, the shrine has been rebuilt many times over the centuries, though elements date back to about 250 years after the Buddha's lifetime. The temple's principal relic is what tradition says is a descendant of the pipal tree (*Ficus religiosa*) under which the Buddha sat. A stone seat called the Vajrasana (Diamond Throne) commemorates the Buddha's meditation cushion. Ritual towers called *stupas* mark the places where the Buddha contemplated his insights.

Monasteries and temples established by Buddhists from Sri Lanka, Thailand, Burma, Tibet, Bhutan and Japan now surround the Mahabodhi Temple complex. A continual stream of international pilgrims visits the site during the cooler months of the year, circumambulating the temple, performing prostrations and offering prayers in a multitude of languages. The sincerity and devotion of these visitors sanctify Bodhgaya as much as the historical events that took place there.

Left The Mahabodhi (Great Enlightenment) Temple in Bodhgaya, India, marks the place where Siddhartha Gautama achieved enlightenment and became the Buddha.

JERUSALEM

Like several of the cities discussed in this chapter, Jerusalem has a multi-layered history, which has made it sacred to various faiths over the centuries. The oldest monuments in the Holy City, dating back to the 10th century BCE, are linked to the Jewish tradition. According to Jewish sources, Jerusalem was founded by ancestors of Abraham and was ruled by the Jebusites until it was conquered by David in around 1000 BCE. David expanded the city and declared it the capital of the unified Kingdom of Israel.

In about 960 BCE David's successor Solomon built the first great Temple on Mount Moriah, which flourished as the centre of Jewish worship for nearly 400 years. In 586 BCE Jerusalem was conquered by the Babylonians led by King Nebuchadnezzar, and the temple was sacked and burned. After several decades of Babylonian captivity, King Cyrus II of Persia allowed the Jews to return to Jerusalem and rebuild their temple. The Second Temple, built over the

'Perhaps the lessons of sacred cities that today lie in ruins can bring to Jerusalem the "heritage of harmony and peace" for which the city is named.'

Right Jerusalem is sacred to three faiths. The Western Wall of the Temple Mount is holy for Jews as a remnant of the Second Temple. To Muslims, the Al-Aqsa Mosque and the Dome of the Rock mark the spot where the Prophet Muhammad ascended to heaven. Christians revere Jerusalem as the site of Christ's Passion.

ruins of the first between 535 and 515 BCE, was destroyed in a Jewish revolt against Roman rule in 70 CE.

Since that time a section of the western supporting wall of the Temple Mount has been the focus of prayer and longing for Jews living in every corner of the world. Jewish law mandates that important prayers be recited facing the direction of the city, and the Western Wall has become the symbol of Jewish unity and national aspiration. Jewish pilgrims fill the city at Passover and other festivals when offerings were historically brought to the temple. Passover prayers that promise 'next year in Jerusalem' are recited around the world in remembrance of this tradition.

For Christians, Jerusalem is the city where Jesus lived, preached, died and was resurrected. The sites of his ministry and of the events of his Passion have drawn devoted pilgrims for centuries. During Holy Week leading up to Easter, Christian pilgrims from around the world carry palm branches as they walk the Via Dolorosa past the 14 stages of the Cross, the route through the old city that Jesus is said to have taken on the way to his Crucifixion.

Pilgrims from the Greek Orthodox tradition travel to the Holy Land so that they can prepare for a good death. In Jerusalem they purchase white funeral shrouds, which they wear when they renew their baptism in the River Jordan, and which they will wear once more when they are buried. At Easter the most important moment for Greek Orthodox pilgrims is the Ceremony of the Holy Fire, when they wait in darkness in the Church of the Holy Sepulchre, above Christ's tomb, for the moment of Resurrection, when candles are lit and passed from hand to hand.

Islam, too, lays claim to Jerusalem. According to the Qur'an, the Prophet Muhammad was miraculously transported from Mecca to Jerusalem. The Al-Aqsa Mosque marks the place where his journey ended. Near by is the Dome of the Rock, built on top of the Temple Mount in the late 7th century, from which Muhammad ascended to heaven accompanied by angels and was then returned safely to Earth. Since that time Jerusalem has been venerated as the third most holy city to Muslims, after Mecca and Medina.

Over the next centuries Jerusalem was the site of bloody religious battles between its Muslim rulers and the Christian Crusaders who marched on the city to take control of its holy places. These religious wars foreshadowed the sectarian conflicts that rock Jerusalem to this day. Perhaps the lessons of sacred cities that today lie in ruins can quell the violence and bring to Jerusalem the 'heritage of harmony and peace' for which the city is named.

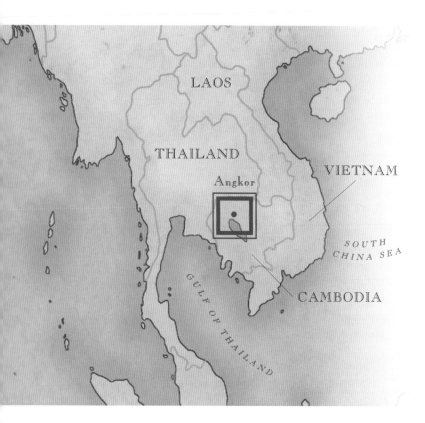

Angkor – Cambodia's temple city

Angkor was the site of a series of capital cities built by the kings of the Khmer Empire of Cambodia between the 9th and 15th centuries. Though the houses, palaces and other structures where people lived and worked were built of wood and other perishable materials and have not survived, more than 1,000 magnificent stone temples are scattered through the forests and rice fields.

The multitude of impressive temples spread over the site are capped by Angkor Wat – an architectural and spiritual masterpiece and the world's biggest single religious monument.

MYTHOLOGY AND RELIGION
The ancient Khmer kings claimed descent from the union of a banished Hindu prince and a 'serpent-woman', the daughter of Nagaraja, the serpent king of the land. As this myth suggests, the Khmer are a joining of Indian Hindu people who migrated to the area and native Cambodian people.

The religious history of the Khmer also links different elements in a snake-like sacred dance. The two great Indian religions, Hinduism and Buddhism, were practised at Angkor sometimes side by side and sometimes during alternate eras. Angkor's sacred monuments began as Hindu temples, but after the middle of the 12th century the Khmer kings embraced Mahayana (northern-school) Buddhism. King Jayavarman VII (ruled 1181–1218) made Mahayana Buddhism the official religion of the empire. The temples built

during his reign celebrated the healing powers of Lokeshvara, a form of the Buddha of Compassion.

However, the successors to Jayavarman VII decided to return the Khmer court to Hindu practice. Some Buddhist sculptures were defaced or reshaped, and the temples once again became Hindu places of worship. In the 13th century, though Hinduism was the official religion of the Khmer court, Theravada (southern-school) Buddhism coexisted peacefully alongside. Over the first quarter of the 14th century Theravada Buddhism was adopted by the Khmer rulers and their people, a final spiritual twist that hastened the end of the Khmer Empire.

COLLAPSE AND REDISCOVERY
The kings of Hindu Angkor had claimed a direct link to the divine world with its omnipotent gods. Under Theravada Buddhism, however, the gods were no longer all-powerful and kings could not base their power on a royal religious cult.

As Angkor weakened as a unified power, so a rival empire grew in strength. During the 14th and early 15th centuries the

powerful army of Siam repeatedly attacked the Khmer capital. In 1432, following a siege, the Khmer royals abandoned Angkor, though the area continued to be inhabited by an agrarian population.

Some temple sites were maintained as Theravada Buddhist shrines; others were abandoned and reclaimed by the forest. Although it was neglected after the 16th century, Angkor Wat was never completely abandoned. The moat surrounding the temple also provided some protection from the jungle. In 1863 Angkor came to the attention of the West when Henri Mouhot, a French naturalist, published a description of the ruins. Scientific expeditions followed, mainly under the auspices of the École Française d'Extrême Orient, founded in 1899, which played a major role in the research, conservation and restoration of Angkor monuments until the 1970s.

CURRENT RESEARCH
Current archeological research at Angkor is based on the most advanced contemporary methodology. A comprehensive aerial survey of the site was carried out by American NASA

Right Restoration work
at Angkor's Ta Prohm
temple is complicated
by 150 large trees
growing among the
ruins, the roots of
which have penetrated
foundations and, in
some cases, enveloped
temple buildings.

spacecraft in September 2000, as part of a joint project by the University of Sydney and ASPARA, the Cambodian agency responsible for Angkor. The remote-sensing images are helping researchers determine the extent and distribution of settlements at Angkor and allowing them to map the effects of current environmental changes as a way of understanding how the same patterns might have contributed to the empire's historical collapse. In particular, scientists are studying whether extensive clearing of forest areas for rice cultivation has contributed to severe flooding in the region.

Work has also been carried out to restore some of the monuments, now deluged by tourists. Collapsed sections of Angkor Wat have been repaired, and in 2005 a Japanese team restored the north library of the outer enclosure. Work is also proceeding on the restoration of Angkor's Ta Prohm temple complex, built in the 12th century by Jayavarman VII. Here work is complicated by 150 large trees that are growing in the complex, the roots of which have penetrated the foundations and dislodged the stones of walls, vaults and towers.

Angkor Wat

The southernmost temple of Angkor's main religious sites, Angkor Wat (wat is the Khmer word for 'temple') was built during the first half of the 12th century in the reign of Suryavarman II (ruled 1113–c. 1150). Dedicated to the Hindu god Vishnu, the temple is a representation of Mount Meru, the abode of the gods in Hindu cosmology. Its five towers, arranged in a quincunx pattern (one in each corner and one in the middle), symbolize the five peaks of the sacred mountain, while the surrounding walls and moat represent mountain ranges and cosmic oceans.

Angkor Wat is surrounded by a moat 190 metres (625 feet) wide, an apron of open ground measuring 30 metres (100 feet) and an outer wall 4.5 metres (15 feet) high. The moat and wall are 5.5 km (3½ miles) in overall length. The area enclosed by these boundaries is a rectangle of 82 hectares (203 acres), within which lay the main temple as well as secular buildings, including residences and, to the north of the temple, the royal palace.

The architecture of Angkor Wat has been praised for its harmony and proportion, and compared favourably with the temples of Greece and Rome. Many design elements, such as the towers shaped like lotus buds and the ornamented galleries, can still be seen, but other features have been destroyed by looting or the passage of time. Originally, the towers and many figures on the bas-relief carvings were decorated with gilded stucco, and the ceiling panels and doors were made of carved wood. Much of the temples' stone ornamentation is still intact, including large-scale bas-reliefs of mythological narratives that have been praised as the greatest known examples of linear stone carving.

① SANDSTONE CAUSEWAY

The main entrance to Angkor Wat was via a sandstone causeway that was constructed to the west of the complex. The causeway runs on top of earth fill and forms a processional way 8 metres (26 feet) wide. Paved with sandstone blocks, it is bordered by *naga* (serpent-shaped) balustrades.

② MAIN TEMPLE

The temple itself is raised on a vast terrace covered with sugar palms and mango trees. The structure consists of three rectangular galleries rising to a central tower, with each level higher than the last. The two inner galleries have towers at the corners surrounding the central tower. Unlike most Khmer temples, this temple is oriented to the west rather than the east. Experts believe that this orientation indicates that Suryavarman II intended the temple to be his tomb and funerary monument, since rituals take place in reverse order during Hindu funerals. This view is supported by the fact that the bas-reliefs on the inner walls of the galleries are intended to be read in an anticlockwise direction, rather than the traditional clockwork progression. The reliefs show scenes from the Hindu epics, the *Ramayana* and *Mahabharata*, as well as historical scenes from the reign of Suryavarman. A spectacular relief on the southern gallery graphically depicts the 32 hells and 37 heavens of Hindu mythology.

③ CHURNING OF THE SEA OF MILK

On the inner wall of the south wing of the east gallery is Angkor's most famous bas-relief, called the Churning of the Sea of Milk. This depicts a Hindu myth in which gods and demons cooperate to churn the primordial ocean in order to produce *amrita*, the elixir of immortality. The *asuras* (demons) pull the front half of a cosmic snake, while the *devas* (gods) pull the rear half. In the centre the snake is wrapped around Mount Mandara, held in place by the Hindu god Vishnu, which serves as a pivot. The back-and-forth motion of this tug-of-war churns the ocean.

④ BAKAN

The innermost gallery of the temple is a 60 metre (200 foot) square known as the Bakan. The gallery's roof is decorated with the repeated motif of the body of a snake ending in the heads of lions or garudas (divine birds). Carved lintels and pediments decorate the entrances to the galleries. The temple's principal sanctuary was at the centre of this gallery and originally held a statue of Vishnu. When the temple was converted to Theravada Buddhism, the open sides of the gallery were walled in and the new walls featured reliefs of standing Buddhas.

⑤ PREAH POAN

On the west side of the temple is a cloister known as Preah Poan, the 'Hall of a Thousand Buddhas'. Over the years Buddhist pilgrims erected a great number of statues of the Buddha in this hall, made of stone, wood or metal. Some of the statues have now been removed. On the pillars of the hall are inscriptions dating from the 16th to 18th centuries recording the good deeds done by pilgrims and members of the royal family. Written in Khmer as well as Burmese and Japanese, they give the authors' 'vows of truth' and declare their faith in the Buddha and his teachings.

⑥ RESERVOIR AND MOATS

The reservoir and moats that encircle the whole temple complex represent the cosmic oceans that surround the world in Hindu cosmology. The moats measure 5.5 km (3½ miles) in overall length. Water, with its life-giving and purifying qualities, is central to Hindu beliefs. A Sanskrit inscription compares the reservoir and moats at Angkor with the tributaries of the sacred Ganges River in India. The moats can be crossed at only two places: to the east at a simple bank of earth and to the west by the sandstone causeway.

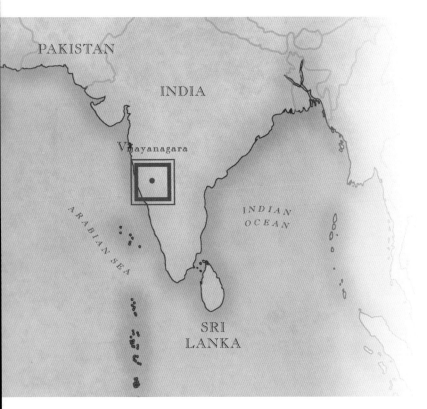

PAKISTAN

INDIA

Vijayanagara

ARABIAN SEA

INDIAN
OCEAN

SRI
LANKA

Vijayanagara – city of temples and festivals

Vijayanagara – the name means 'Victory City' – is the ruined capital of the Vijayanagara Empire that ruled much of southern India from the early 14th to the mid-16th century. Laid out along the southern bank of the Tungabhadra River, the sacred centre contains Vijayanagara's principal temples, including the exquisite Virupaksha Temple, which is still in use today.

In the metropolitan area as a whole there are more than 140 sacred sites linked to Hindu myths and legends, which make Vijayanagara an important destination for festivals and pilgrimages.

TEMPLES AND SACRED SITES

The sacred centre of Vijayanagara consists of two temple districts. Temples sacred to the Hindu god Vishnu are primarily sited to the east, while the temples sacred to Shiva are located to the west. The most important of the Shiva temples is the Virupaksha. This temple dates to the 9th or 10th century, predating the Vijayanagara Empire. The temple is dedicated to Virupaksha, an aspect of Shiva, and his consort Pampa, a beautiful local maiden.

According to legend, Pampa worshipped Shiva with great devotion, attracting the attention of the god, who offered to marry her. The stages of their betrothal and marriage are celebrated in a series of annual festivals. A November festival marks their engagement, during which the gods are serenaded as their barge is rowed around the temple tank. Two chariots are pulled

through the streets of the village of Hampi during the wedding festival in April. Pilgrims attend both festivals and pay homage to Virupaksha and Pampa throughout the year, as they have done since the days of the Vijayanagara Empire.

Another important Vijayanagara temple is the Vitthala, dedicated to a form of the god Krishna. This shrine is noted for its wonderfully artistic animal carvings and the large carving of a stone chariot or *ratha*. Carved out of a single rock, the chariot is

THE MAHANAVAMI FESTIVAL

At the height of the Vijayanagara Empire, Persian and European visitors to the court gave vivid descriptions of life in the capital, including accounts of the annual nine-day Mahanavami Festival. According to Portuguese trader Domingo Paes, who visited Vijayanagara in about 1520, the festival included processions of animals, warriors and noblewomen, as well as contests of skill such as wrestling matches. It concluded with fireworks and a military review.

Though the Vijayanagara kings were not considered to be divine, their authority was based on their perceived ability to maintain cosmic order. To underscore their connection with divine power, the Vijayanagara kings played a central public role in the Mahanavami festivities. Pavilions were set up for visitors within the royal district of the capital, images of the gods were brought to the city and presented to the king, and temple dancers celebrated his royal authority.

itself a miniature temple. In addition to temples, Vijayanagara has many smaller sacred sites. Small shrines are everywhere, images of deities are carved into boulders and rock slabs and there are many statues of gods and goddesses. Folk traditions are also honoured, as in the piles of naga stones, sacred to the serpent king.

FALL, RESTORATION AND RESEARCH

The Vijayanagara Empire was often in conflict with Muslim kingdoms to the north. In 1565 an alliance of these kingdoms succeeded in defeating the empire's army and the capital was captured. Over the next months Vijayanagara was destroyed and its population scattered. Though the ruined city was never rebuilt or repopulated, the Virupaksha Temple remained a sacred site. At the end of the 18th century it was renovated and refurbished, and public festivals in honour of Virupaksha and Pampa resumed.

Archeological work on the ruins dates back to a visit that the British antiquarian Colin Mackenzie, the future Surveyor General of India, made in 1799. He mapped the whole site, commissioned watercolour paintings of the ruins and collected manuscripts for study. Several photographs taken in the 1850s and 1860s document the historical condition of Vijayanagara's temple ruins. With the publication in the 19th and

Above This chariot, a miniature temple, is among the exquisite carvings at the Vitthala temple, sacred to the Hindu god Krishna. Its stone wheels, each shaped in the form of a lotus, are capable of revolving.

early 20th centuries of various books about Vijayanagara, such as *The Forgotten Empire* by Robert Sewell, a civil servant in colonial India, interest in the site grew. Work at the site is now carried out by the Vijayanagara Research Project, which has been clearing and excavating it since 1980.

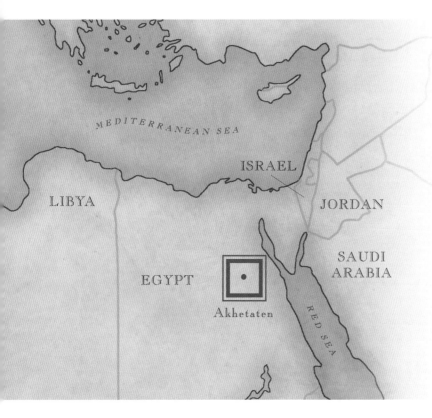

Akhetaten – city of the sun

Akhetaten is the capital constructed by the 18th-dynasty Egyptian pharaoh Akhenaten, who ruled from 1353 to 1336 BCE. He was a religious revolutionary who single-handedly converted Egyptian worship to a form of monotheism. In the first year of his reign he proclaimed that the only god was Aten – the sun-disc itself, the energy that is the source of all life.

When Akhenaten died, his new capital city with its public buildings, Aten temples, palaces and homes was abandoned just 20 years after it was built, and Egypt returned to its familiar pantheon of gods and goddesses.

HORIZON OF ATEN

Akhenaten began construction of Akhetaten – the city's name means 'The Horizon of the Aten' – in the fourth year of his reign. By year nine, the city was completed. Located on the east bank of the Nile 312 km (194 miles) south of Cairo, Akhetaten (more commonly known today as el-Amarna) was a virgin site, designed and built from the ground by the Pharoah. The extent of the city was marked by 14 boundary stelae – decrees carved on tablets embedded in the cliffs on either side of the river. The inscriptions on the stelae give a vivid account of the pharaoh's selection and dedication of the site of his capital.

Akhetaten's central city contained the Royal Palace, the Great Temple of Aten, the Small Temple of Aten, as well as a number of government and public buildings. The Aten temples differ from other Egyptian temples in that Aten was worshipped in the open sunlight, rather than in an inner enclosure housing a cult statue. The city also included residential areas for officials, workshops for stone-carvers and other artisans, grain silos and bakeries, common homes built of mud bricks, gardens, a number of zoos and several necropolises (tombs).

Little of the city now remains. When Akhenaten died, the cult he had founded fell out of favour. In the second year of his reign, his son and successor, Tutankhaten, changed his name to Tutankhamun and abandoned the capital that his father had built. Tutankhamun's successors dismantled the temples and other buildings Akhenaten had constructed and used the stone and building materials for their own temples. So thoroughly did later pharaohs wish to eradicate his heretical beliefs that they eliminated Akhenaten and his immediate successors from the official list of pharaohs. It was not until the end of the 19th century that his identity was rediscovered and the surviving traces of his capital were unearthed by archeologists.

Above *This family scene shows Akhenaten, his queen Nefertiti, and three of their children. In the centre, the sun god Aten bathes the royal family in sacred rays.*

***Right** This granite statue in the Egyptian Museum in Cairo shows Akhenaten in the Amarna style, noted for its elongated forms and exaggerated features but also for its harmony, proportion and unique beauty.*

NEFERTITI

The artistic style that was developed during Akhenaten's reign was as revolutionary as the Pharaoh's innovative religion. The statues, carvings, busts and wall paintings from this period are unique in Egyptian art for their realistic portrayal of their subjects. Rather than being shown in idealized portraits, Akhenaten and his wife Nefertiti are depicted in informal scenes, such as playing with their children. Nefertiti also appears beside the king, suggesting that she enjoyed unusual power for a queen. Other reliefs show her riding in a chariot with Akhenaten, kissing him in public and even sitting on his knee.

Nerfertiti's beauty was renowned in the ancient world. A bust of the queen, one of the most famous icons of ancient Egyptian art, was found in the studio of the sculptor Thutmose by German archeologists who excavated at Akhetaten in the years prior to the First World War. The bust is now housed in Berlin's Egyptian Museum.

The residence that is popularly called the Palace of Nefertiti features other realistic artworks. A central chamber on the north side of the palace, known as the Green Room, was painted with a continuous frieze that depicts the natural life cycle of the marshes. It features paintings of birds, some of which are diving into the marshes for prey. The palace also had a central sunken garden for birds, a terrace bordered with trees and zoological gardens, and a ceiling that may have served as a trellis for vines.

THE AMARNA LETTERS

The first map of Akhetaten was prepared by experts who were travelling with Napoleon between 1798 and 1799. Other early visitors to Akhetaten sketched the reliefs and monuments that they found there. Beginning in 1891, scientific excavations were carried out by a series of British and German teams. However, a most significant find was made in 1887 by a local woman, who uncovered a cache of more than 300 cuneiform tablets. Known as the Amarna Letters, they record diplomatic correspondence between Akhenaten and officials in other Egyptian cities.

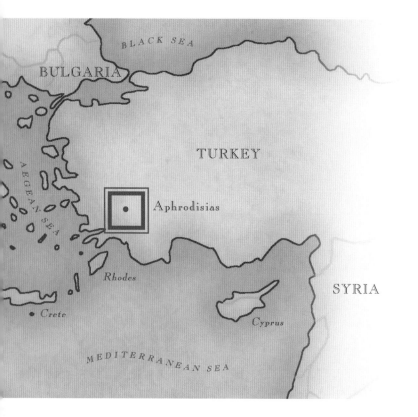

Aphrodisias – city of the goddess of love

Aphrodisias, named for Aphrodite, the Greek goddess of love, was one of the most important pilgrimage places of the Greek and Roman period in Turkey. The city was set among rolling hills and surrounded by cypress groves, 230 km (140 miles) south-east of Izmir. The focal point was the magnificent Temple of Aphrodite, built in the late 1st century BCE and the early 1st century CE.

Like many other goddess temples, the site was originally sacred to the ancient Mother Goddess, and the temple was later was converted into a Christian basilica.

SCULPTURES AND MONUMENTS

Excavations indicate that the site of Aphrodisias was settled from at least the 5th millennium BCE. Long before the Temple of Aphrodite was built, the city was considered a holy spot. One of the original names of the city was Ninoe, which probably refers to the Mother Goddess Nin, known elsewhere in the ancient world as Astarte or Ishtar.

In the late 1st century BCE Aphrodisias came under the personal protection of the Roman emperor Augustus, and the city became a wealthy and important trade centre. In addition to the famous temple, it was noted particularly for the excellence of its school of marble sculpture. Quarries from which beautiful white and blue-grey marble could be cut lay about 1.6 km (1 mile) east of the city. Sculptured portraits of important citizens and of Greek gods and Roman emperors decorated the public buildings. Excavation of a sculptor's workshop in the

1960s yielded stone-carving tools, 25 half-finished statues and practice pieces carved by apprentices. Statues made in Aphrodisias were exported as far away as North Africa and Rome.

Monuments in the town include a large *agora* (public square), originally enclosed by *stoas* (porches); the lavish Baths of Hadrian, with five barrel-vaulted chambers richly decorated with sculptures; the Bouleuterion, the city council chamber, which was used for musical performances as well as public meetings; and the Sebastion, a temple used to celebrate the imperial cult of Augustus, which was discovered in 1979. The city's stadium, one of the best preserved from the Classical era, seated 30,000 spectators and hosted athletics competitions and festivals in Roman times.

TEMPLE OF APHRODITE

Built over the ruins of earlier sanctuaries, the Temple of Aphrodite followed an octastyle design, with eight columns on the front and rear and 13 columns on each side. As in other temples dedicated to Aphrodite, worship probably included ritual sexual

encounters with priestesses and *hierodules*, or temple women. The *cella* (inner chamber) of the temple housed the cult statue of Aphrodite, a version of which is displayed in the Aphrodisias Museum. The statue's stiff frontal pose is reminiscent of other Anatolian goddess figures, such as the Artemis of Ephesus (see pages 166–169). The front of her formal robe, which conceals her body, is carved with reliefs that symbolize aspects of Aphrodite's divine identity and mythological power.

Around 500 CE, during the Byzantine era, the temple was converted into a Christian basilica. Columns from the front and back were moved from their original positions

Right *The Temple of Aphrodite once had eight columns at the front and rear and 13 columns at the sides. Inscriptions on some columns record the contributions of important citizens of Aphrodisias to the shrine's construction.*

and used to extend the side colonnades, creating two long rows of 19 columns each. The cella was dismantled and the stone reused in the construction of new walls. Similar conversions of goddess sites into churches can be seen all over the ancient world.

COLLAPSE AND CURRENT RESEARCH

Because of the great popularity of the city's goddess cult, paganism continued to linger at Aphrodisias well into the Christian era. However, the major earthquakes that took place during the 4th and 7th centuries damaged the monuments of Aphrodisias and the town fell into disrepair. Arab raids, political and economic pressures and epidemics all also led to further decline. In 1402, after an attack by Tamerlane, the Turkish-Mongolian warlord who conquered much of central Asia, the site of Aphrodisias was completely abandoned.

The ruins of Aphrodisias have been explored since the early 18th century. Currently research is being carried out by archeologists from New York University. Among the new techniques being employed is a virtual re-creation of the city's agora, in which artificial intelligence is used to determine the movements of the characters living inside the virtual city, offering viewers a more realistic experience of life in the ancient town.

'The focal point is the magnificent Temple of Aphrodite, once the pre-eminent temple of the goddess in Asia Minor.'

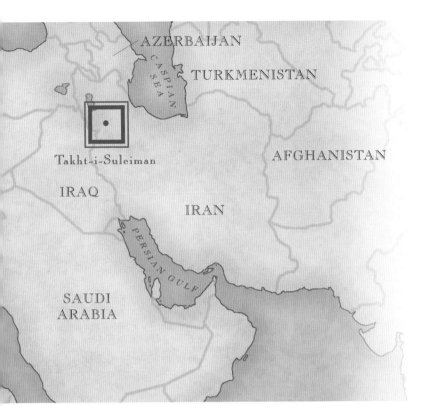

Takht-i-Suleiman – Zoroastrian fire temple

Takht-i-Suleiman – the name means 'Solomon's throne' – is the holiest pre-Islamic site in western Azerbaijan, 400 km (250 miles) west of Tehran in Iran. The ruins are set in a valley surrounded by volcanic peaks on the shore of a mineral-rich lake believed to be bottomless.

The ruins date to the Parthian (250 BCE–226 CE) and Sassanid (226–650 CE) dynasties of Persia, and the site has a long sacred history. An ancient volcano about 3 km (2 miles) west of the ruins is known as Zendan-i-Suleiman, 'Solomon's prison'. Legend says that King Solomon used to imprison monsters inside its crater. North of the volcano, about 8 km (5 miles) from the ruins, is a mountain also called Takht-i-Suleiman, where Solomon is said to have built a summer palace for the Queen of Sheba. The site also includes the ruins of Adur Gushnasp – an ancient city and fire temple that is one of the three Great Fires of the Zoroastrian faith.

THE FIRE TEMPLE

When A.V. Williams Jackson (1862–1937), the first professor of Indo-Iranian Languages at Columbia University in New York City, visited the site in 1906, he published a detailed description of the ruins and temple. In Jackson's account, the ruined city was once surrounded by massive ramparts, 9–12 metres (30–40 feet) high, with huge gateways aligned to the cardinal compass

THE GREAT FIRES

Zoroastrianism is an early form of monotheism based on the teachings of the sage Zoroaster (sometimes called Zarathustra), who lived around 600 BCE. Fire is sacred to Zoroastrians as a symbol of Ahuramazda – proclaimed by Zoroaster to be the one uncreated Creator of all. Zoroastrian scriptures state that the Great Fires have existed since creation and were brought forth to propagate the faith, dispel doubt and protect humankind. Nearly every town had a sacred fire, as does every Zoroastrian temple. Of the three Great Fires, one was sacred to priests, one was sacred to farmers and one – the fire at Adur Gushnasp – was sacred to warriors and kings.

According to Arab historians, all of the fire temples built in Persia obtained their holy fire from the sacred flame at Adur Gushnasp, which was traditionally believed to have burned without interruption for 700 years. The sources say that before Persian warriors embarked for battle, they visited the fire altar at Adur Gushnasp for spiritual strength and guidance. Each potential Sassanid ruler also journeyed there to humble himself at the sacred fire before ascending the throne.

Below *The landscape around Takht-i-Suleiman is imbued with sacred significance. In the distance is an ancient volcano linked by legend to King Solomon. The lake in the foreground is said to be bottomless.*

points. The fire temple itself was an arched and vaulted building with a dome, made from bricks nearly 30 cm (12 in) square. Entrance to the temple was through two arched portals, from which worshippers descended to a vaulted brick chamber below that had walls 1.2–1.5 metres (4–5 feet) thick. Inside the chamber were arched wall recesses. In Jackson's view, the whole temple had the feel of a place built expressly to preserve a precious treasure.

FALL OF THE SASSANID DYNASTY

Though the site of Adur Gushnasp had been considered holy for centuries, the fortified city and temple were refurbished and improved by the most famous Sassanid king, Khosrau I (ruled 531–579 CE), a great builder and administrator. Though he decreed that Zoroastrianism was the official religion of his state, Khosrau was tolerant of all faiths and even allowed one of his sons to become a Christian.

Khosrau II (ruled 590–628 CE), the grandson of Khosrau I, was a much less successful ruler than his illustrious predecessor had been. His expansionist military campaigns over-extended the Persian army and over-taxed the Persian people. With his empire weakened from 15 years of war, Khosrau II was defeated in 627 at the Battle of Nineveh, when Byzantine emperor Heraclius (ruled 610–641 CE) sailed up the Black Sea to attack Persia from the rear. Heraclius' army then marched through western Persia, sacking and burning Persian cities, including Takht-i-Suleiman. Soon after the defeat, Khosrau was assassinated and chaos and civil war followed. Though the city and temple were rebuilt and remained in use during the Mongol Empire, by the 13th century the site was completely abandoned.

REDISCOVERY

In 1819 Robert Ker Porter, a British diplomat, painter and traveller, rediscovered the site and produced a careful collection of sketches and drawings that recorded what he found there. In 1840 Henry Rawlinson, a British scholar, visited the site and was the first to decipher cuneiform inscriptions that suggested that the ruins were the remains of Adur Gushnasp.

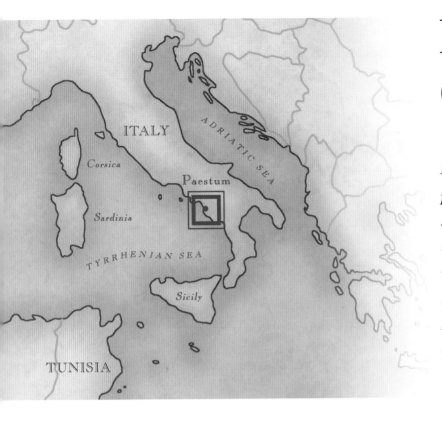

Paestum – Italy's Greek temples

Paestum is a major Greco-Roman city on the Italian plains south of the Amalfi coast, some 80 km (50 miles) south of Naples. It was originally called Poseidonia, after Poseidon, the Greek god of the sea. The city is renowned for its Doric-style Greek temples, considered to be the best preserved in the world. The temples to Hera, Athena and Apollo were constructed between 550 and 460 BCE and functioned as places of worship under Greek, Lucanian and Roman rulers.

When Christianity became dominant, the Temple of Athena was converted into a Christian church and remained in use until the 8th century CE.

POSEIDONIA'S TEMPLES AND TOMBS

Founded by Greek colonists in the 7th century BCE, Poseidonia was a peaceful and prosperous city, surrounded by fertile fields and connected by inland trade routes to the Etruscan cities to the north and the Greek cities to the south. Defensive walls surrounded the city, with gates in the cardinal directions. During the city's height, from 600 to 400 BCE, a series of great temples were constructed.

The earliest of these temples to be erected was dedicated to Hera, the wife of Zeus. Built in the archaic Doric style in 550 BCE, it was part of a large enclosed sanctuary to Hera that included other temples and altars. Devotion to Hera (or, under Roman rulership, to Juno) involved bringing gifts to the temple, such as small terracotta female statues. The gifts were then buried in consecrated pits.

The second temple, to Athena, was built on the highest point of the city in around 500 BCE. It is the first-known temple to combine Doric-style columns in the main peristyle (the colonnade surrounding the temple's interior court) with Ionic-style columns on the porch. A main altar stands in front of the temple to the east, where votive offerings could be presented to Athena (Minerva to the Romans).

The god honoured at the third temple, built *c.* 470–460 BCE, has been disputed by experts. Some believe that it was a new temple to Hera; others that it honoured Neptune, the Roman equivalent of Poseidon. Still others cite offertory statues found around the main altar as indicating that the temple was dedicated to Apollo. It is the largest of the three temples and is beautifully preserved.

Left *The Temple of Athena is the second of the great temples at Paestum. Built on the highest point in the city, as Athena temples usually were, the temple features both Ionic and Doric columns.*

Poseidonia's ruins also include several necropolises. Some of the tombs were painted on the inside walls. What is now called the Tomb of the Diver has the most interesting artwork. The inside of the lid of the tomb has a painting of a man diving into the water from a tall structure, as if he were diving into the afterlife.

NEW RULERS

Around 400 BCE Poseidonia was conquered by the Lucanians, an indigenous people who lived in the mountainous areas further inland. Except for the change of rulers, life in Poseidonia continued unchanged. Greek was the spoken and written language, and the temples and their cults continued to be venerated. However, in 273 BCE Lucania

fought for the losing side in the Third Samnite War, and Poseidonia became a Roman colony. The new rulers changed the name of the city to Paestum, killed or enslaved the citizens and remodelled the city's architecture on Roman style. The temples, however, remained unchanged. Rededicated to the Roman gods, they continued to be used and maintained.

The city's decline came about gradually. Shifting trade routes weakened the economy, and environmental changes that affected the city's water supply turned the land around Paestum into swamps. The loss of arable land and the spread of diseases such as malaria reduced the population. With the coming of Christianity, people moved to the high ground around the

Athena temple, which was transformed into a church. But by the 8th century the town was practically abandoned.

EXCAVATION

Though Paestum's temples were known, they were not studied until the discovery of Pompeii in the mid-18th century stirred interest in Italy's classical past. Scientific excavation did not begin until the early 20th century, and art treasures such as the paintings in the Tomb of the Diver were not discovered until the late 1960s. Even today, only a small fraction of the original area of the city has been excavated. Major parts of Paestum are privately owned, and a road built across the site in 1930 buried the northern half of the city.

Left *The Temple of Hera is an archaic Doric temple that has been dated to 550 BCE based on its style. It was part of a larger enclosed sanctuary dedicated to Hera called the Heraion that included several minor temples and altars.*

'The inside of the lid of the Tomb of the Diver has a painting of a man diving into the water from a tall structure, as if he were diving into the afterlife.'

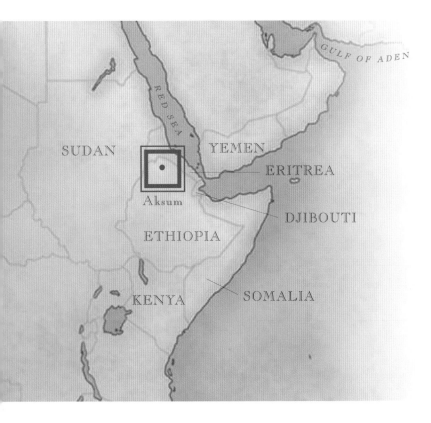

Aksum – holy city of Ethiopia

Aksum was the chief city of a kingdom that flourished in the Ethiopian highlands near the Red Sea from c. 1–700 CE. The people of Aksum were descended from an indigenous people who spoke Kush and a Semitic people from southern Arabia. Aksumites erected impressive monoliths and practised a unique form of Christianity. The city's most venerated possession is what many people believe is the Ark of the Covenant.

This object has ensured that Aksum's Church of St Mary of Zion and the Treasury, where the Ark is kept, are major destinations for pilgrims.

THE MYSTERY OF THE ARK

The legendary Ark of the Covenant is a portable box-like shrine constructed at the time of Moses to carry the tablets upon which God had inscribed the Ten Commandments, given to Moses on Mount Sinai. Some accounts say that the wooden chest was lined, inside and out, with pure gold and topped with winged cherubims. Eventually the Ark was installed in the innermost sanctuary – the Holy of Holies – in the great Hebrew temple in Jerusalem. At an unknown date the object vanished and wound up, some say, in Aksum. According to Ethiopian legend, the Ark was stolen from Jerusalem by the companions of Menelik, son of the Queen of Sheba and King Solomon. Menelik brought the Ark to his home city of Aksum, where it has remained ever since.

During the 4th century, the Aksumite king converted to Christianity and built the first church of St Mary of Zion on the foundations of ancient pagan temples. This church stood for hundreds of years and was considered by the travellers who saw it to be particularly grand and noble. In the 1500s the church was destroyed by Muslim raiders, but it was rebuilt in 1635 and this building still stands today. The church's square structure shows Syrian influence. It has fortress-like walls decorated with colourful murals and paintings. A modern church completed in 1964 serves today's pilgrims. Between the two churches is a fenced and guarded building – the Treasury – built in 1965 by Ethiopian emperor Haile Selassie to house the Ark.

Left *Destroyed and rebuilt several times, the church of St Mary of Zion standing today was built in 1635. In front of the church is the Coronation Stone where emperors of Ethiopia traditionally came to be crowned.*

ABYSSINIAN CHRISTIANITY

Aksum's original religion was polytheistic, but when its king converted to Christianity, he declared Aksum to be a Christian state. Adhering to a tradition with Egyptian roots, Aksum's Christians believed that Christ had a single nature (his human nature merged with the divine) rather than a dual nature (simultaneously human and divine). This view was branded as heretical in 451, but is still held by Abyssinian (Ethiopian) and Coptic Orthodox Christians.

Aksum's practice of Christianity has several other unique features. In the 5th century Aksumites replaced the Greek liturgy with their own native language, Ge'ez. In the 6th century Aksum conquered several small Jewish kingdoms in Arabia and incorporated some Jewish customs into its religious practice. Because of their Semitic ancestors, the people of Aksum believed they were descendants of King David and were thus appropriate inheritors of the Ark of the Covenant.

Aksum began to decline during the 7th century after the rise of Islam, because of the growing power of Muslim Arabs throughout the Middle East. Arab traders took control of key routes, and Aksum faded from international importance. But in the early days of Islam, a group of followers of Muhammad were given asylum from persecution in Aksum. For this reason the city was not forcibly converted to Islamic practice, and the Abyssinian Church has lasted until the present day.

Below No one has yet proved conclusively the age and purpose of the granite obelisks near St Mary of Zion, but it has been suggested that they were built as memorial stelae.

THE GRANITE OBELISKS

Near the church of St Mary of Zion is a group of towering obelisks – large slabs of stone carved with mysterious designs. They are the tallest single pieces of stone quarried and erected in the ancient world. The tallest obelisk stands 33.3 metres (109 feet) high and weighs 5 tonnes. It probably collapsed as it was being erected and lies in six massive pieces. The tallest standing monolith measures 23 metres (75 feet). The age of the obelisks and their purpose have not been conclusively determined, but the presence of burials near by has led experts to believe that they were intended as memorial stelae. In 1937 an obelisk 24 metres (80 feet) tall was cut into three parts and shipped to Rome to be re-erected. After a long dispute, it was returned to Aksum in 2005.

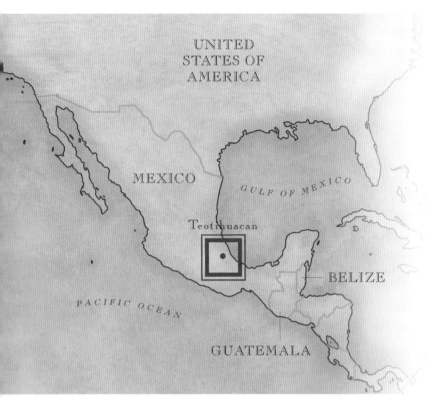

UNITED
STATES OF
AMERICA

MEXICO

GULF OF MEXICO

Teotihuacan

BELIZE

PACIFIC OCEAN

GUATEMALA

Teotihuacan – Mexico's place of the gods

The city of Teotihuacan flourished in the valley of Mexico, 40 km (25 miles) from Mexico City, between the 1st and 8th centuries. Since no written histories of Teotihuacan are known and no writing system has been discovered, almost all that is known about what was once the largest city in Meso-America has come from studying the ruins.

Even the original name of the city is unknown. Teotihuacan, which means 'the place of the gods' in Nahuatl, was named by the Aztecs some 700 years after the city's mysterious collapse. The Aztecs also named Teotihaucan's monumental Pyramids of the Sun and Moon and regularly visited the site as a place of pilgrimage.

MONUMENTAL SACRED ARCHITECTURE

Teotihaucan's massive stepped pyramids, ceremonial avenues and plazas established a pattern that influenced the art and architecture of later Mayan and Aztec cities. Its main thoroughfare, named the Avenue of the Dead by the Aztecs, is aligned precisely in accordance with the heavens and the surrounding landscape. A sight line directly over the top of the Pyramid of the Moon at the north end of the Avenue of the Dead is oriented 15.5 degrees east of north and aligns with the mountain peak of Cerro Gordo. Bisecting the city, the Avenue of the Dead functioned as a grand processional way. It is interspersed with small plazas and lined with dozens of small stepped

platforms, temples, altars and apartment complexes for priests or other elite citizens.

The Aztecs associated the Pyramid of the Moon with their moon and water goddess Chalchiuhtlicue. The four-tiered pyramid stands 46 metres (150 feet) high and can be ascended from a south-facing stairway. The plaza in front of the pyramid is surrounded by smaller stepped platforms and buildings decorated with well-preserved carvings and murals depicting jaguars, serpents, butterflies, eagles and ornately attired priests or gods. As with other monuments in Teotihuacan, rituals and beliefs associated with the Pyramid of the Moon are unknown.

The city's most impressive monument, the Pyramid of the Sun, lying to the east of the Avenue of the Dead, is aligned to the place on the eastern horizon where the sun rises at the spring equinox. Originally comprising four stepped tiers, the massive structure measures more than 200 metres (650 feet) on a side and stands 63 metres (208 feet) tall. A monumental stairway ascends the west face of the pyramid. Recent excavation has uncovered a sacred cave beneath the structure, which the Aztecs associated with

their own creation myths as 'the place where time began'. The entire structure seems to have symbolized the cosmic mountain of creation, which one ascends in order to come into the presence of the gods.

The ritual heart of the city was the Ciudadela (citadel) – a massive plaza where it has been estimated that more than 100,000 people could gather for ritual events. Dominating the plaza is Teotihaucan's most important monument, the Temple of the Feathered Serpent. All four sides of the temple's façade are adorned with carved heads of the Feathered Serpent – an early form of the Aztec god Quetzalcóatl, also associated with the influential early Meso-American city of Tula (see pages 132–133). Excavations have discovered the graves of more than 200 people attired as Teotihuacan warriors who were sacrificed when the temple was dedicated.

COLLAPSE AND EXCAVATION

At the city's height, between 150 and 450 CE, approximately 200,000 people lived in Teotihuacan, making it the largest city in the Americas and one of the biggest in

the world. Its decline was dramatic and mysterious. Around 700 CE, Teotihaucan's main ceremonial monuments and buildings were burned. Earlier archeologists believed that the city was destroyed by invaders, possibly the Toltecs. But recent evidence shows that the destruction was limited to the city's temples, palaces and homes of the elite citizens, indicating that the burning was due to an internal uprising. Further evidence correlates the city's decline with climate changes leading to drought and famine, perhaps made worse by over-population. By

the end of the 8th century, Teotihuacan was largely abandoned.

Knowledge of the site was never lost, but the first scientific excavation was not carried out until the early 20th century. The Pyramid of the Sun was restored in 1910 to celebrate the centennial of Mexican independence. Current excavation by Mexico's National Institute of Anthropology and History, focused on the Pyramid of the Moon and the Temple of the Feathered Serpent, is still expanding our knowledge of the culture of this influential Meso-American city.

Above *The Aztecs named Teotihaucan's ceremonial avenue and main thoroughfare the 'Avenue of the Dead'. Like the stepped Pyramid of the Sun (to the left of the avenue), it is aligned precisely with the surrounding landscape and the heavens.*

Ephesus – city of Artemis and the apostles

Ephesus was one of the great cities of ancient Asia Minor. Located on the coast of the Mediterranean in Anatolia (modern Turkey), it was founded, according to legend, by the Amazons, a nation of female warriors. Famed in antiquity for the Temple of Artemis, one of the Seven Wonders of the ancient world, Ephesus later played an important role in the history of Christianity.

The apostles John and Paul both lived in the city of Ephesus. In 431 CE, during the meeting of the Third Ecumenical Council in Ephesus, Mary was officially proclaimed the Mother of God.

THE TEMPLE OF ARTEMIS

What is known about the earliest temples to the goddess who was worshipped at Ephesus comes from historical sources. The first shrine was probably built around 800 BCE. Though the Ionian Greeks who colonized Ephesus identified the goddess with Artemis, their virgin goddess of the moon and the hunt, the goddess of Ephesus has more in common with the Mother Goddess of Minoan Crete (see pages 140–141). Her cult statue – its torso covered with what have been interpreted as breasts, eggs or even bulls' testes – symbolizes abundance and fertility. The earliest temple may have contained a sacred stone rather than a statue, probably a meteorite.

By 600 BCE Ephesus had become a major trading port. The architect Chersiphron was commissioned to build a new temple, which he did on a grand scale. The structure had a double row of Ionian columns on the long sides and three rows on the shorter sides. The colonnade surrounded a walled court, in which was situated the shrine housing the cult statue. This temple was destroyed in around 550 BCE when Ephesus was conquered by King Kroisos of Lydia. When peace was restored, King Kroisos contributed towards building a new temple, as is shown by fragments of inscribed column bases.

The new temple, the next-to-last to be built at Ephesus, was larger than its predecessor. It boasted 100 stone columns supporting a massive roof. It was this temple that was mentioned by various Greek historians as one of the Seven Wonders of the ancient world. Historical sources report that it was burned down in 356 BCE by a man named Herostratus, who did so to have his name go down in history. Traditionally the temple was burned on the night that Alexander the Great was born in Macedon. The Roman historian Plutarch says that the goddess was too busy taking care of the birth

'Though the Ionian Greeks identified her with the virgin goddess Artemis, the goddess of Ephesus has more in common with the Mother Goddess of Minoan Crete.'

of Alexander to save her temple. The citizens of Ephesus were so appalled at this arson that they decreed that anyone who spoke of Herostratus would be put to death.

When Alexander the Great came to Ephesus in 333 BCE, a new temple (the last dedicated to Artemis) was still under construction. In 1863 the British Museum in London sent architect J.T. Wood to Ephesus to search for the Temple of Artemis. Despite many obstacles and hardships, he finally found the base of the temple at the bottom of a muddy test pit, 6 metres (20 feet) deep. Fragments of column drums, which may have been carved by the famed sculptor Skopas, were excavated in the late 19th and early 20th centuries and are displayed in London's British Museum.

CHRISTIAN EPHESUS

According to some traditions, after the Crucifixion the apostle John took Mary under his protection and brought her with him on his travels to spread Christianity in Asia Minor. Documents from the Third Ecumenical Council repeat the tradition that St John and the Virgin Mary lived at Ephesus. St John's Basilica was built in the 6th century over the supposed site of the apostle's tomb.

St Paul visited Ephesus twice on his travels through Anatolia. In 57 CE a silversmith named Demetrius gave a rousing speech in opposition to Paul's attempt to convert the Ephesians to Christianity. The speech ended with the words, 'Great is Artemis of the Ephesians.' In the end, however, Christianity won out. By the time the final Temple to Artemis was destroyed by the Goths in 262 CE, both the city and worship of Artemis were in decline.

Right *Column drums and foundation stones from the last Temple of Artemis in Ephesus. It seems fitting that Mary was proclaimed Mother of God in a city where the Divine Feminine had been honoured since antiquity.*

Ephesus

In Roman times Ephesus was the capital of proconsular Asia. Many of the most beautiful buildings of Ephesus, the ruins of which can be seen today, date to this period. The city thrived from rich commerce and a brisk sea trade. Immigrants from many nations flocked there, swelling the population to more than 200,000.

In April huge crowds of visitors filled the city for the Festival of Artemis, during which statues of the goddess were carried in procession and plays were performed in the theatre. The Roman city's boast that it was 'the first and greatest metropolis in Asia' had the ring of truth.

The Temple of Artemis at Ephesus was discovered by the Victorian architect J.T. Wood. Further expeditions in the early 20th century found evidence of several temples at the site, each constructed on top of the previous one. According to Roman historian Pliny the Elder, the last temple to be built there was 130 metres (425 feet) long and 68 metres (225 feet) wide, with 126 columns. Said to be the first temple constructed completely of marble, it was lavishly decorated and filled with artwork, including four bronze statues of Amazon women.

Another important structure in Ephesus was the Temple of Hadrian, which was constructed between 117 and 138 CE to honour the emperor Hadrian, who visited Ephesus in 128. The façade features four Corinthian columns supporting a curved arch. Inside the temple above the door is a relief of Medusa keeping watch. Friezes on the interior walls tell the story of the mythical founding of Ephesus, and include images of the Amazons and various Greek gods and heroes.

① HARBOUR

By Roman times the harbour at Ephesus, the city's vital link to maritime commerce, had begun to silt up because the Cayster River continually carried silt into it. Roman engineers rebuilt the harbour, dredged it and, as a last resort, changed the course of the river. Despite these efforts the entrance to the sea was ultimately pushed 4 km (2½ miles) to the west. The resulting loss of trade contributed to the city's decline.

② THE GREAT THEATRE

Located on the slope of Panayir Hill opposite Harbour Street, the Great Theatre is the largest classical theatre in Anatolia. An earlier Greek theatre was enlarged and improved during the reigns of Roman emperors Claudius (41–54 CE) and Trajan (98–117 CE). The façade of the three-storey proscenium (enclosure for the stage) was richly decorated with columns, reliefs and statues. The theatre's 66 rows of seats could accommodate some 24,000 patrons for concerts, plays, religious events and gladiator spectacles.

③ SACRED WAY: MARBLE ROAD AND CURETES STREET

From the Theatre, the Sacred Way wound through Ephesus to the Temple of Artemis. The first section of it, from the Theatre to the Celsus Library, is called Marble Road. It dates from the 1st century. Beneath the marble pavement was the city's elaborate water and sewer system. The portion between the Library and the Hercules Gate is called Curetes Street, named for a class of priests mentioned in many inscriptions.

④ CELSUS LIBRARY

This beautiful structure was built in 135 CE to house the tomb of Gaius Julius Celsus Polemaenus, Roman governor of the province of Asia. His tomb lies beneath the ground floor and the two upper storeys were a library with reading rooms. More than 12,000 manuscript scrolls were kept in cupboards in niches in the walls. The façade was decorated with Corinthian columns and wall niches holding statues of Sophia (wisdom), Episteme (knowledge), Ennoia (intelligence) and Arete (virtue).

⑤ COMMERCIAL AGORA

This colonnaded public square was built in the early 3rd century to replace an earlier Greek trading site. Three gates led into the square: from the harbour, the Great Theatre and the Celsus Library. Shops lined the covered portico that surrounded three sides. At the centre of the square were a sundial and a water-clock.

⑥ ODEON

This small theatre was used as a city council chamber. It was built during the 2nd century by wealthy citizens Publius Vedius Antoninus and his wife Flavia Papiana. The theatre was probably roofed and seated 1,400. It was used for concerts when the council was not in session.

⑦ ARCADIAN AVENUE

Leading from the harbour to the Great Theatre, this important avenue was lined with columns and shops decorated with statues. At night, it was illuminated with candle street lamps. Originally constructed during the Hellenistic period, the avenue was restored in Roman times by Emperor Arcadius (ruled 395–408 CE).

⑧ VEDIUS GYMNASIUM

This school was built during the 2nd century by Publius Vedius Antoninus and his wife Flavia Papiana. It offered instruction in art, sports, drama, speech and literature. The courtyard was surrounded by columns and the main hall, the Hall of Emperors, was embellished with statues and a mosaic floor.

⑨ STATE AGORA

Built during the 1st century BCE, this public space was used for governmental discussions. It had colonnaded porticoes on three sides and in the centre a temple dedicated to the Egyptian goddess Isis. The temple's façade was decorated with statues depicting the legend of Odysseus and the Cyclops Polyphemos. During the reign of the Emperor Augustus (ruled 31 BCE–14 CE), the temple collapsed and was not rebuilt.

Epidauros – Greek healing sanctuary

Epidauros was an ancient Greek city in the eastern Peloponnese, 125 km (80 miles) south-east of Athens. It was the site of the most celebrated centre for healing in the ancient world. The Asklepieion, the sanctuary of Asklepios, the Greek god of healing, was used to treat ills of the body, mind and spirit with a combination of recreation and ritual.

Right *The lovely setting and acoustics of the great open-air theatre at Epidauros are remarkable. The whispered words of an actor standing at the centre of the stage can be heard by a person sitting in row 55, the uppermost row of the audience.*

Drama was considered therapeutic, so Epidauros boasts the most perfect classical theatre in Greece. The principal ritual that took place at Epidauros was a kind of dream healing, in which people slept together in a holy chamber, hoping to receive a dream pointing to a cure.

THE HEALING PROGRAMME

Pilgrims who visited Epidauros seeking a cure could take part in a comprehensive programme of healing activities. As the ruins indicate, a variety of structures were included in the curative environment. There was a stadium where spectators enjoyed games of skill and strength, a gymnasium for lectures and philosophical discussions, baths for purification and a superb open-air theatre where musical performances and plays uplifted the mind and purged the emotions through catharsis: the combination of pity and fear at the emotional heart of Greek drama.

After refreshing the mind and body through these activities, supplicants needing special healing took part in a dream healing ritual. Having engaged in purification, prayer and sacrifice, participants entered the Abaton – a long, narrow building where they spent the night hoping for a visitation from Asklepios, the divine physician. Snakes may have played a part in the ritual. Ancient accounts say that sacred snakes actually licked or touched affected body parts to accomplish a cure. In other cases the god sent a dream that indicated what steps should be followed to bring about healing. Many carved tablets describing miraculous cures were found during the archeological excavation of the Abaton.

MONUMENTS AND EXCAVATION

The earliest structures at Epidauros date back to the 6th century BCE. Among the monuments that have been excavated are the Propylaia, a small temple at the ancient entrance of the site. The Greek inscription over the doorway ends with the words 'Think holy thoughts', a reminder that healing necessitates rebalancing the mind and spirit as well as the body.

The Temple of Asklepios had six fluted Doric columns at each end and 11 columns on each side. Its decoration was elaborate and brightly coloured. The cella (inner

sanctuary) housed a huge gold and ivory statue of Asklepios, carved by Thrasymedes of Paros. The most impressive and beautiful building at Epidauros is the Tholos, a round structure with two concentric circles of columns designed by famed Greek architect Polykleitos in the 4th century BCE, whose ancient purpose is still debated by experts. Recent excavations have revealed that the Tholos was built over a small stone labyrinth accessible from a trapdoor in the cella. It is possible that supplicants were led into the labyrinth in a ceremony simulating a visit to the underworld, before being healed into a new life.

The great theatre at Epidauros was praised for the beauty of its architecture even in ancient times. Also designed by Polykleitos, its plan and proportions are based on the principles of sacred geometry. The theatre's acoustics are still astounding: as the Epidauros tour guides are delighted to demonstrate, the whisper of a person standing in the centre of the orchestra (the site of the ancient altar) can be heard even in row 55, which is the uppermost row of the seating area. The theatre's setting in a lush landscape that can be seen over and around the stage area contributed to the health-enhancing experience of the audience – and still does, when plays are performed in the space each summer.

ASKLEPIOS AND GREEK HEALING

In Greek myth, Asklepios was the son of the god Apollo and of Coronis, a beautiful mortal woman. Jealous because Coronis had taken a mortal lover, Apollo ordered that the child be exposed on a mountaintop near Epidauros. Later the child was raised by the wise and gifted centaur (half-man and half-horse) Chiron, who taught Asklepios the art of healing.

So skilled a healer was Asklepios that he brought back to life a mortal who had died. This angered Zeus, who struck Asklepios down with a lightning bolt. Cult statues of Asklepios show him holding the staff of life around which a snake is entwined. The snake, which renews itself by shedding its skin, links Asklepios with the natural processes of regeneration.

Index

Acknowledgements

akg-images 39, 91; /British Library 34; /ullstein bild 25. **Alamy**; /Jon Arnold Images 144; /Ian M. Butterfield 155; /Djuric Dejan/Diomedia 167; /Larry Dunmire/Photo Network 99; /geogphotos 37; /Images of Africa Photobank/Nick Greaves 105 bottom; /Wolfgang Kaehler 12-13; /Craig Lovell/Eagle Visions Photography 94; /Duncan McNeill 38; /Mediacolor's 45; /Panorama Media (Beijing) Ltd. 8; /Beren Patterson 77; /Simon Reddy 153; /Jack Stephens 43; /World Pictures 16. **Bridgeman Art Library**/Biblioteca Nazionale Centrale, Florence, Italy, 110; /Boltin Picture Library 114; /Ilya Glazunov/Private Collection 17; /Royal Geographical Society 93; /Viking Ship Museum, Oslo, Norway/Giraudon 24. **www.catalhoyuk.com** 57. **Corbis** 59, 100; /Lynsey Addario 52; /Dave Bartruff 162; /Annie Griffiths Belt 71; /Yann Arthus-Bertrand 103; /Bettmann 154; /Jonathan Blair 145; /Christophe Boisvieux 29; /Christie's Images 116; /Dean Conger 51, 139; /Richard A. Cooke 95, 165; /Tony Craddock/zefa 64-65; /Macduff Everton 19, 101; /Werner Forman 128; /Michael Freeman 10; /Darrell Gulin 67; /Lindsay Hebberd 15; /Jeremy Horner 76; /Eric and David Hosking 44; /George H. H. Huey 73; /Archivo Iconografico, S.A. 78, 84; /Mimmo Jodice 79; /Wolfgang Kaehler 53, 157; /Catherine Karnow 142-143; /Earl & Nazima Kowall 68; /Bob Krist 112-113; /JP Laffont/Sygma 147; /Patrice Latron 75; /David Lees 40-41; /Charles & Josette Lenars 6; /Michael S. Lewis 106-107; /Michael Nicholson 140; /Diego Lezama Orezzoli 58; /Gianni Dagli Orti 23, 117; /David Reed 105 top; /Roger Ressmeyer 11; /Fulvio Roiter; /Roman Soumar 146; /Keren Su 88-89; /Reza/Webistan 47; /Tim Thompson 18; /Alan Towse/Ecoscene 70; /Vanni Archive 125; /Gian Berto Vanni 115; /Ruggero Vanni 170-171; /K. M. Westermann 55; /Roger Wood 85; /Alison Wright 49; /Jim Zuckerman 149, 160. **www.foxybiddy.com**/Lynne Newton 69. **Getty Images**/AFP 9; /DeA Picture Library 129; /Robert Harding World Imagery 135; /Sisse Brimberg 161. **Franck Goddio**/Hilti Foundation/Christop Gerigk 33. **Martin Gray**/sacredsites.com 21, 158-159, 163. **Hellenic Ministry of Culture**/23rd Ephorate of Prehistoric and Classical Antiquities. **Lonely Planet Images**/Izzet Keribar 27. **South American Pictures** 92. **Still Pictures**/Michael J. Balick 111. **Superstock**/age footstock 119, 123; /Silvio Fiore 126-127; /Newberry Library 61. **Hugh Thomson 2003** 109. **Werner Forman Archive** 83.

Executive Editor Sandra Rigby
Project Editor Fiona Robertson
Executive Art Editor Sally Bond
Designer Elizabeth Healey
Illustrator Lee Gibbons
Picture Researcher Jennifer Veall
Production Controller Audrey Walter